A GREAT WEEKEND IN

BERLIN

A GREAT WEEKEND IN
BERLIN

The first thing that will strike you upon arrival in Berlin is the forest of cranes, scaffolding and enormous machinery that has dominated the city since reunification. Together they offer the unusual image of an urban landscape in the process of transformation. This is a city caught between the recent past and a future, in the process of forging a new history.

Impressive for its enormous size, long avenues and vast open spaces, Berlin is a city in the process of developing a new identity. With its low population density, many lakes and forests, river and canals, parks and gardens,

mechanism in a city which, throughout the 20th century, was the scene of sudden and violent destruction and which has experienced the ups and downs of history like few others. You won't be able to miss the signs of this

it in some ways resembles a provincial town, which means that Berliners are spared much of the stress of other large cities.

It is said that the Berliners can be bad-mannered and occasionally even aggressive, but their attitude, which is often called Prussian, must be considered a defence

during your stay, from the Neue Synagoge desecrated and destroyed during Kristallnacht in 1938, to the red line drawn on the ground in the Mitte district which serves as a reminder that the Wall once stood here. Despite this side to their character, the Berliners are also renowned for their tolerance and sense

of humour. Berlin has an air of freedom where everyone can dress and live as they please. It wasn't just by chance that in the 1970s, 80s and 90s the punk, alternative and techno movements found fertile ground for their expression here, more than in any other city in Germany. These movements gave birth to a unique, vibrant underground culture attracting young anti-establishment protesters, and artists from around the world. The latter have formed groups in the Kreuzberg district, the heart of the alternative movement, where you'll move between squats, art galleries and welcoming *Kneipen* (pubs), and Prenzlauer Berg, where the young avant-garde like to meet in the fashionable cafés and clubs.

The impertinence, originality and eccentricity of these movements (the most striking example of which in the last few years has been the Love Parade) have their roots in

the 1920s. This period was an explosion of amazing artistic expression, brutally cut short by Nazism, that the Berliners, since the fall of the Wall, would fervently like to revive. Their wish may become reality, as since reunification Berlin has seen the emergence of an ambitious young inter-national contemporary art scene. The city is also endowed with a large quantity of museums, housing many masterpieces and superb art collections, and you'll need more than just a weekend to explore the riches of the Museuminsel, Kulturforum and Dahlem. Aside from these large museums, there are a considerable number of theatres, concert halls and opera houses, some of which are world-famous These include the celebrated

Philharmonie, home to the Philharmonic Orchestra that for a long time had Herbert von Karajan as conductor. In other words, the city possesses a formidable cultural heritage that it seems able to integrate and maintain in the face of major financial difficulties. It has to be said that few cities in Europe are as fascinating as Berlin. With its past history, plans for the future, lively, eccentric underground culture, intense nightlife and multicultural, cosmopolitan character, the new capital of Germany is both captivating and surprising. Since 1989, the city has had to cope with the difficult consequences of reunification and the problems this has brought. Today, East and West Berliners regard each other with a certain wariness which can be explained by their history, the rise in unemployment and by the loss, for all, of a number of privileges. It will be a few years yet before the disparities and the animosity between Wessi (the inhabitants of the old West) and Ossi (the inhabitants of the old East) disappear. Yet, with all these contrasts and contradictions, Berlin is an excitng place to live, to visit, to go out in and to have fun in, an unusual city that fascinates and questions, but never leaves you indifferent.

How to get there

Berlin is on the northenmost edge of western Europe. If you dislike harsh, icy winters and baking hot summers, the best time to go there is in the spring or autumn. The climate at these times is mild and the skies are clear and blue — ideal weather for walking, sightseeing and getting to know the city.

WHEN TO GO

The harsh winters (with frequent snowfalls and temperatures that can fall to as low as -15°C/-26°F) can make the city grey and miserable. However, Berlin is worth visiting over Christmas and the New Year, when there are huge celebrations with masses of decorations and Christmas markets. Once the mild spring weather is past, the intense summer heat gives the city a holiday air, with everyone rushing to swim in the lakes or to sunbathe and picnic in the parks. Luckily, a sea wind from the Baltic ltakes the edge off the heat. Whatever the season, there can be sudden showers or changes in temperature, so be prepared.

HOW TO GET THERE

Even if you are live in Europe, the most quickest and economical way of getting to Berlin is by plane. Travelling by bus is a cheaper option, but the journey from anywhere outside Germany is long and arduous.

BY PLANE FROM THE UK

British Airways
☎ 0345 222 111
www.britishairways.com
Flies direct from London to Berlin.

Buzz
☎ 0870 240 7070
www.buzzaway.com
Flies direct to Berlin and offers some of the lowest fares out of the UK.

Virgin Express
☎ 020 7744 0004
www.virgin-express.com
Another relatively cheap

option, Virgin flies direct from London to Berlin.

FROM IRELAND
Virgin Express
☎ 020 7744 0004
www.virgin-express.com
Flies direct from Shannon.

FROM THE USA AND CANADA
At the moment flights from Berlin from outside Europe fly via other German or European cities, however, this is bound to change over the next few years.

British Airways
www.britishairways.com
Flies from major US airports via London.

Delta Airlines
www.delta-air.com
Flies from major US cities via Paris or Frankfurt.

FROM AUSTRALIA AND NEW ZEALAND
Singapore Airlines
☎ 02 9350 0100
www.singaporeair.com
Flies from New Zealand and Australia via Singapore.

Cathay Pacific
☎ 13 17 47 (free call)
www.cathaypacific.com
Fly daily from Sydney via Hong Kong.

BY TRAIN
If you're already in Europe and time is not of the essence, the train is also an option although it's not much, if at all, cheaper than flying. From London the journey time via Brussels is 11 hours, from Paris it's 12 hours and 40 minutes. In the UK call:
☎ 020 7387 0444
(www.europeanrail.co.uk) for train tickets for travel all over Europe. Ask about their discounted rates if you're under 26.

FROM THE AIRPORT TO THE CITY CENTRE
Berlin has three airports: Tegel, Tempelhof and Schönefeld. Western European flights, as well as flights from Australia, New Zealand and the US land at Tegel or Tempelhof – Tegel, which lies north-west of the city, is the largest and most recent. To get to the city, you have to catch a 128 bus to Kurt-Schumacher-Platz (U6) U-Bahn (underground)

INCLUSIVE BREAKS

Many tour operators offer two and three-day weekend breaks that include travel (by plane, train or coach) and accommodation in various categories of hotel. For the best rates, you have to spend Saturday night in Berlin. In a city where accommodation is expensive, the main attraction of these breaks is that they give you the chance to stay at a luxury hotel for a very reasonable price. You also benefit from the rates negotiated by tour operators and travel more cheaply while avoiding the bother of booking.

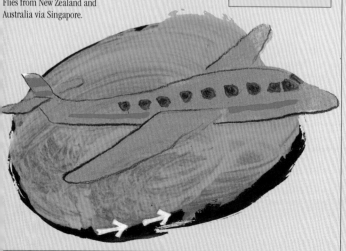

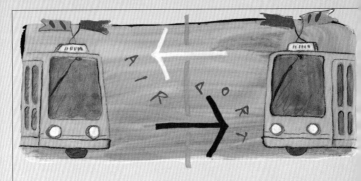

station or a 109 bus, which will take you to Zoologischer Garten. Buses leave the airport every 10 minutes from 5am to 11pm. Tickets cost DM3.90 on the bus or from machines in the arrivals hall. A taxi ride to Bahnhof Zoo costs DM25-30 and takes 15 minutes. The second airport, Tempelhof, a historical monument altered under the Nazi regime, is right in the heart of the city. You can reach the centre of Berlin in 20 minutes by 119, 184, 341 or 104 bus. You can also take a taxi

renovations have changed the direction of traffic-flow and created bottlenecks, making driving in the city more difficult. Try to avoid driving in the Kurfürstendamm, Unter der Linden, around the Postdamer Platz building site and in Moritzplatz. Apart from these affected areas, and once the rush hour (5-7pm) is over, traffic flows relatively freely in Berlin. You'll find a wide choice of car hire companies around Alexanderplatz, especially in Karl Liebknechtstraße.

FORMALITIES AND VISA REQUIREMENTS

If you are a citizen of the European Union, all you will require to enter the country is a valid identity card or passport. If you are travelling from the US, Canada, Australia or New Zealand, and are staying for less than three months, you will not require a visa.

CUSTOMS

EU nationals over 17 years of age do not need to declare goods imported in or exported

(which takes 10 minutes and costs DM20) or walk to Tempelhof U-Bahn station.

CAR HIRE

Given the size of the city, it isn't necessarily a bad idea to hire a car. However, for the last three or four years, large numbers of building sites and

USEFUL ADDRESSES

Embassies (at home)
UK: 23 Belgrave Square
London SW1X 8PZ
☎ 020 7824 1300
🆕 020 7824 1435

US: 4645 Reservoir Road
Washington DC 20007
☎ 202 298 4000
🆕 202 298 4249

Canada: 1 Waverly Street
Ottowa, Ont. KP2 OT8
☎ 613 232 1101
🆕 613 594 9339

Australia: 119 Empire Circuit
Yarrkumla ACT 2600
Canberra

☎ 02 6270 1911
🆕 02 6270 1951

Tourist Offices (at home)
UK: P.O. Box 2695,
London W1 3TN
☎ 020 7713 0908
🆕 020 7714 6129

US: 122 E 42nd Street
Chanin Building 52nd Floor
New York, NY 10168
☎ 202 298 4000
🆕 202 298 4249

Canada: 175 Bloor St East
North Tower, Suite 604
Toronto, Ont. M4W 3R8
☎ 416 968 1570
🆕 416 968 1986

Australia: 1st Floor,

36 Carrington St
Sydney NSW 2000
☎ 02 9299 3621
🆕 02 9299 3808

Consulates in Berlin
UK: Unter den Linden 32-43,
☎ 201 840

Ireland: Ernst-Reuter-Platz 10,
☎ 261 11 61

US: Neustädtische
Kirchstrasse 4-5,
☎ 238 51 74

Canada: Friedrichstrasse 95,
23rd Floor ☎ 261 11 61

Australia: Uhlandstrasse
181-183, ☎ 880 08 80

from Germany. Non-EU citizens are allowed to import 200 cigarettes or 50 cigars or 250g tobacco, 1 litre spirits or 2 litres wine, 50ml perfume, 500g coffee, 100g tea, other goods to the value of DM350 for non-commercial use. The import of meat, fruit, plants, flowers and protected animals is restricted or forbidden. Non-EU citizens may buy duty-free goods to export to their home country, but there are limits and your home country will have set allowances. To find out what these are, contact your local customs office:

US Customs Service
☎ 202 927 6724

Revenue Canada
☎ 800 461 9999

Australian Customs Service
☎ 02 9213 2000

New Zealand Customs Service
☎ 09 359 6655

INSURANCE

UK tour operators are obliged by law to offer insurance covering loss of possessions and health and repatriation insurance but not cancellation and luggage insurance. If you pay for your plane or train ticket with an international credit card, you're automatically entitled to good cover for medical expenses and the cost of repatriation (although it is advisable to check what's on offer before you travel). Otherwise, it's best to take out cover for the cost of repatriation with a reputable insurance company

HEALTH

If you're on a course of medical treatment, take enough medicine with you when you go in case you can't find the same one in Berlin. Citizens of European Union countries should obtain form E111 from their local post offices before departure and will then be entitled to free medical assistance. In the event of an emergency, all you have to do is go along to one of the AOK (German Social Security) centres in Berlin to exchange your E111 form for a *Krankenschein,* which you then present to a doctor or at the emergency department of a hospital.

AOK (for foreigners)
Hohenzollerndamm, 183,
10713 Berlin, Wilmersdorf
Train: U2-U7 Fehrbelliner Platz
Mon.-Wed. 8am-3pm,
Tue.-Thu. 8am-6pm,
Fri. 8am-noon.

CURRENCY AND CASH

Germany is one of the European Union countries that has already joined the single currency, and from 2002, the German Deutschmark (DM or 'mark') will be replaced by the Euro. In the meantime, all prices are listed in both marks and euros.

A mark is divided into 100 pfennigs. There are 1, 2 (still in use!), 5, 10 and 50 pfennig and 1, 2 and 5 mark coins, and 10, 20, 50, 100, 200, 500 and 1,000 mark notes (though most shopkeepers are reluctant to accept 500 and 1,000 mark notes).

It isn't necessarily advantageous to buy marks

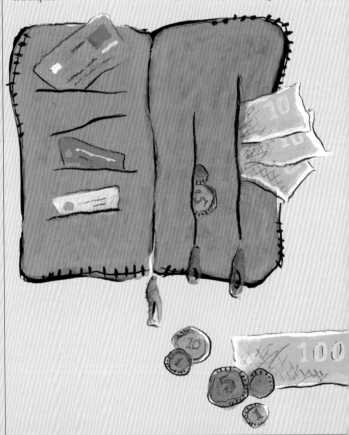

before departure, since the exchange rates and commissions are more or less the same in both countries. The banks in Berlin have very irregular opening hours, which vary in different branches and districts, but they are usually closed on Saturdays. If you can, change your traveller's cheques and cash at the bureaux de change in stations and airports, which offer a good rate of exchange and are open until late at night and at the weekend. Money can also be changed at certain post offices. Germans in general and Berliners in particular are wary of credit cards (until the fall of the Wall, Visa cards weren't accepted in Berlin) and it's therefore a good idea to carry cash, traveller's cheques or Eurocheques as well, which are more likely to be accepted in shops and restaurants, especially in the old East. However, things are changing rapidly, so make a point of asking if cards are accepted. There's no problem where cash machines are concerned. There are very few nowadays that don't accept all international credit cards (for a small commission, of course!).

BUDGETING FOR YOUR STAY

Since the war and until reunification, Berlin was relatively affordable, if not cheap, compared to some European capitals and other cities in Germany. Accommodation aside

(it's hard to find rooms for under DM100), the cost of living is still reasonable today. You can expect to pay DM2.50-3 for a coffee and DM3.50-5 for a beer. The well-known *Currywurst mit Pommes* costs at most DM4.50. By comparison, a public transport ticket seems quite expensive (DM3.90). It isn't unusual to get a filling meal for as little as DM12 in *Kneipen* or small local restaurants . For something more sophisticated, you generally won't have to pay more than DM35. Cultural activities can be very affordable, especially if you're entitled to reductions. A museum ticket costs DM4-12, a concert or theatre ticket costs DM15-50, or as much as DM120 for certain operas, and entrance to a club or disco costs DM10-20, not including a drink. Once you've paid for transport and accommodation, DM150 a day is enough to cover meals and outings.

LOCAL TIME

Germany is one hour ahead of Greenwich Mean Time. Summertime starts at the end of March, when clocks are put forward an hour, and wintertime at the end of September, when clocks go back an hour.

VOLTAGE

The current in Germany is the same as in Britain (220 volts). However, Germany has two-way plugs and sockets rather than three, so you'll need to take an adaptor with you or buy one at the airport.

JAYWALKING

In Germany – and Berlin is no exception – jaywalking is against the law and is a fineable offence. You will find that nearly all Germans respect this law. If you ignore it you may incur a fine of DM20, or at the very least receive some very disapproving looks.

LOST PROPERTY

If you lose anything on public transport contact the BVG Fundbüro at:

Potsdamer Strasse 180-82
Schöneberg 10783
☎ 25 62 30 40.

Otherwise you should contact the nearest police station. Remember to always report any thefts or losses in order to be able to claim on your insurance when you get home.

LIBRARIES

Books in English are available at the following libraries, however, unless you become a member of the library, you will not be able to take books from the premises.

Staatsbibliothek
Potsdamer Strasse 33
Tiergarten 10773
☎ 20 15 2
Train: S1, S2/U2
Open Mon.–Fri. 9am–9pm,
Sat. 9am–7pm.

British Council
Hardenbergerstrasse 20
Charlottenburg 10623
☎ 31 10 99 10
Train: S3, S5, S7, S9?U2
Open Mon., Wed., Thur.-Fri.
2–6pm, Tue. 2–7pm.

BERLIN, THE CITY OF THE WALL

The most senseless construction of the 20th century, the Berlin Wall, wasn't only a symbol of the cold war, it was above all a physical and psychological wound for the city and its inhabitants. For years relatives, friends, neighbours and colleagues were separated from each other. Only a few scattered remnants of the 'Wall of Shame' remain, however, in spite of its almost total disappearance, it's still present in the minds of Berliners.

A LITTLE HISTORY

After the Second World War, the victors each appropriated a share of Germany. The country and its capital were divided into four occupation zones – British, French, American and Soviet. Tension soon grew between the Soviets and their allies over Berlin, culminating in the blockade of the city by the Soviet Union in 1948. The British and Americans immediately responded by organising a giant airlift lasting nine months that supplied the Western sector of the city. Once the blockade

was lifted, East Germany progressively severed communications with the West and nipped any early resistance in the bud. In the 1950s, many East Germans chose to escape repression in their country by fleeing to West Berlin, where they could still cross over the border. Despite more and more stringent checks, the exodus to the West increased steadily over the years. To stem this flood of emigrants, the GDR – backed by the Soviet Union – decided on 13 August 1961 to shut off the city by enclosing West Berlin within a wall. Thus the construction of this senseless barrier was begun.

GLASNOST AND A TIME OF CHANGE

For many years, the two separate parts of the city were virtually independent of one another. Official contact between east and west was virtually non-existent. However, in the mid-1980s, a new openness on the part of Moscow – *glasnost* – heralded a change. The GDR, for its part, preferred to maintain the policy of total separation. Faced with the growing number of protest movements, and after a procession of over a million people through the streets of East Berlin on 4 November 1989, the country's leaders were eventually obliged to give in.

9 NOVEMBER 1989

On 9 November 1989 at 6pm, a Party secretary announced in a terse press release the unconditional delivery of visas to those wishing to cross the border. The news spread fast and, within a few hours, the small groups gathered at the checkpoints became crowds. Faced with the onslaught, the border guards opened the gates. A human tidal wave swept through the gates into West Berlin to shouts of welcome and tears of joy. That same night, young pacifists armed with hammers and chisels began to break down the Wall. By the end of 1990, it had been completely destroyed. On 3 October 1990, Germany was reunified and on 20 June 1991, the city once again became the capital and seat of the government of a united Germany.

HAUS AM CHECKPOINT CHARLIE

This museum opened in 1963 on the site of the famous East-West crossing point, Checkpoint Charlie and provides detailed information on the history of the Wall. Friedrichstrasse, 44, Kreuzberg ☎ 253 72 5 0, open every day 9am-10pm. The East Side Gallery in Mühlenstraße shows sections of the eastern side of the Wall painted after the opening of the borders.

FACTS AND FIGURES

The Wall encircled West Berlin and had a total length of 155km/97 miles, for 43km/27 miles of which it crossed the city from one side to another, separating it from its eastern part. Built mainly of 4m/13ft-high concrete slabs, the Wall was reinforced on the eastern side, with a 6-7m/20-23ft wide wall walk, antitank and antivehicle ditches, 300 control towers and 22 bunkers. In nearly 30 years, the western police recorded 5,043 people (known as 'wall-breakers') who overcame the Wall, an average of one refugee every two days. There were probably more. On the eastern side, 160 people were killed trying to cross the wall and 260 were wounded by bullets. Given that these events were a matter of national security in the GDR, the figures have yet to be confirmed.

THE BIGGEST FRESCO IN THE WORLD

In the west, the Wall soon became the ideal canvas for artists from all over the world. It was initially covered with slogans, posters and tracts by

way of expressing thoughts and feelings, then later, in the 1980s, with graffiti by unknown and famous artists, such as Keith Haring. On the eastern side, the Wall, which could not be approached to within 10m/30ft for fear of being violently forced back or even arrested, was completely painted white.

A CITY OF MUSIC LOVERS

Few cities can pride themselves on offering such a wide range of music to such a large, enthusiastic audience. Berlin's love of music dates back to Friedrich-Wilhelm II (1740-1786), who was not only a monarch and war leader but also a talented flautist and composer. Since his reign, Berlin has constantly played host to the greatest composers, musicians and conductors in the world, including Richard Strauss, Yehudi Menuhin, Arnold Schönberg and Herbert von Karajan, to name but a few.

Herbert von Karajan

A TEMPLE OF CLASSICAL MUSIC

Classical music is undoubtedly the area in which Berlin excels. The city possesses one of the finest concert halls in the world, the Philharmonie (see p. 45), with its legendary acoustics. It was inaugurated in 1963 and is home to the world-famous Philharmonic Orchestra, which had Herbert von Karajan as one of its most illustrious conductors. Since the maestro's death in 1989, Claudio Abbado has carried on the tradition. Since the fall of the Wall, Berlin has boasted no less than eight prestigious symphony orchestras in addition to the Philharmonic Orchestra. These include the Berliner-Sinfonie-Orchester, which is housed in the famous Schinkel Schauspielhaus. Besides the larger venues, the city also has countless other high-quality concert halls. Musical events also take place in churches, castles and there are many open air concerts. In July, the renowned Classic Open Air in Gendarmenmarkt square offers a variety of outstanding concerts.

THE GREAT OPERA HOUSES

Berlin has five classical opera houses to its credit, three of which are world-renowned.

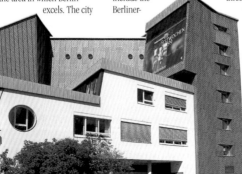

The Deutsche Oper, in the west, dating from 1961, is the youngest but most well established (see p. 124). It shouldn't be confused with the Deutsche Staatsoper, in the east, which is Berlin's oldest opera house (see p. 124). Inaugurated in 1742, it owes its existence to Friedrich II and its current fame to Daniel Barenboim, who has been its conductor since 1992. The less conventional Komische Oper is known throughout the world for the originality of Harry Kupfer's productions and the youth of his company.

VARIETY SHOWS, REVUES AND CABARET

The tradition of variety shows, revues and cabaret dates back to the 1920s. At that time, Berlin was the metropolis of pleasure, with over 150 variety theatres. Since the fall of the Wall, the city seems to be seeking to revive this old tradition. In the last few years, the Theater des Westens has become one of the foremost venues for operettas and musicals in Europe, with the revues of Kurt Weil

SOME MAJOR EVENTS

Berliner Festwochen
One of the most famous festivals of classical music (Aug.–Sep.).

Jazz Fest Berlin
The most renowned jazz festival in Germany, with spots by international artists (Nov.).

Metrobeat at the Kulturbräuerei in Prenzlauer Berg
A forum for Berlin groups featuring all styles of music (Sep.).

Carnival of cultures
Don't miss this big festival dedicated to all the minority cultures, with a parade through the streets of Kreuzberg (May). For more information, contact Berlin Hotline ☎ 25 00 25.

and popular successful stage shows such as *La Cage aux Folles*. With its feather-clad dancers, the Friedrichpalast, built at the time of the GDR, presents itself as 'Europe's biggest revue'. In another vein altogether, the Bar der Jeder Vernunft and the Chamälon appear to have made a success of presenting highly original variety

shows and cabarets that are still entirely in keeping with the times.

A DYNAMIC POP SCENE

Berlin's legendary pop and rock scene is unquestionably the most lively in Germany. It was in Berlin that the eccentric and scandalous Nina Hagen gave her performances. Drawn by the atmosphere and excitement of the city, stars such as David Bowie, Iggy Pop and Nick Cave have come to live here from time to time. It was also in Berlin that some of Detroit's most avant-garde DJs chose to live in the 1990s.

The city is packed with a multitude of original places and more or less official venues where the most varied groups perform on a daily basis. With an endless choice of concerts ranging from drum'n'bass, punk, world music and techno to traditional jazz, experimental and contemporary music, there's something for everyone to enjoy.

THEATRE AND CINEMA

Berlin has nearly a hundred and fifty theatres, including some that are world famous. This may seem to suggest that the city could once again become the theatre capital of Germany, or even Europe, but the reality is quite different. Today, theatres in both the east and the west of the city are desperately competing for funds. Though the situation is critical, it hasn't prevented the rapid rise of a new form of unsubsidised theatre, the 'off' theatres.

These are so dynamic and diverse, that post-war cinema seems moribund in comparison, although the recent spate of successful comedy films is starting to contradict this.

FAMOUS THEATRES

With reunification, Berlin has found itself in possession of a large number of famous theatres, many of which are in the former GDR. The best-known of them all is undoubtedly the Berliner Ensemble, which was founded by Brecht in 1949. Also in the east of the city, the Deutsches Theater enjoys a similar reputation.

Max Reinhardt

It owes its world fame to the actor and director Max Reinhardt, who was its owner until 1933. More modest but just as famous, the Maxim-Gorki-Theater is the main setting for performances of plays from the former USSR and Eastern Bloc countries. The Volksbühne stages outstandingly original productions. Over in the West, the Schaubühne was for a long time considered to be one of the best theatres in Germany (see p. 124).

VARIETY THEATRES

The more popular variety theatres are sometimes in a more fortunate situation than the city's other theatres. There are two variety theatres in West Berlin, but the productions they stage often leave much to be desired. On the other hand, the part-variety, part-classical *Theatre of the Renaissance* has a good reputation. The same is true of the Hansa-Theater, which stages high quality productions in the tradition of popular theatre. The situation in the east is quite different, since almost all the theatres have farces in their repertory and are not keen on variety.

'OFF' THEATRES

In the 1980s, a new form of avant-garde theatre, the 'off' theatre, appeared in West Berlin. With the fall of the Wall, there was a boom in such productions, especially in the east. This part of the city became fertile ground for the new theatre, which had long been forbidden in the GDR. Today, Berlin has well over five hundred so-called 'off' theatres. Many run into financial difficulties and are forced to close down after a while but some, such as the Theater zum Westlichen Stadthirsche, have become institutions.

Metropolis by Fritz Lang

THE BABELSBERG STUDIOS

Berlin isn't only a theatrical city, it's also a city with a long cinema tradition. The famous UFA studios founded in Babelsberg in 1917 saw the birth of masterpieces such as *Metropolis* (1926) by Fritz Lang and *The Blue Angel* (1930) by Joseph von Sternberg, starring Marlene Dietrich. Unfortunately, the Nazis' rise to power put a stop to this. The big stars

emigrated en masse to Hollywood, marking the end of German cinema. After the war, the studios were taken over by the GDR. Now open to the public, they're mainly used for television. Studio tours 6 Mar.-31 Oct. 10am-6pm, ☎ 721 27 50.

A NEW BEGINNING?

Reunification has seen the rebirth of the German cinema, as shown by the spate of successful comedies over the last few years. The film *Run,*

Lola, Run by the young Berlin director Tom Tykwer made quite an impact – not only was it the most successful film in Germany in 1998, it was also the German film most widely shown abroad since *The Drum* by Volker Schlöndorff.

The Blue Angel by Josef von Sternberg

BEER AND SCHNAPPS

It's no secret that the Germans, like their Czech neighbours, love beer. It's been at the centre of their culture since the Middle Ages. There isn't a single town or village that doesn't have its own brewery. Almost all the big festivals centre on beer. Step inside the *Kneipen* and *Gaststätte* and prepare to discover the thousand and one different German beers. *Prost*!

BERLINER WEISSE

Probably imported from Hamburg, the famous Berliner Weiße made its appearance in Berlin around the end of the 16th century. A wheat beer with a bitter flavour, it often needs to be sweetened with raspberry or asperula syrup *(Schuss)* – hence the unusual red *(rot)* or green *(grün)* colour of the brew, which is served in wide glasses. If you go to Berlin over the summer, make sure you try this

summer beer that's as light and sparkling as champagne. Apart from the Weiße – which is more commonly known as *Molle* – there are four other breweries in Berlin, which sell their beer throughout the city. These beers, Engelhardt, Berliner Kindel, Berliner Pilsner, Schultheiß and Bürgerbräu, have a truly unique flavour. Try them all to find your favourite.

A SURPRISING MIXTURE

At festival time, the Germans are in the habit of drinking a glass of *Schnaps* to help them digest their beer.

Schnapps is a generic term that designates a whole range of spirits made in northern Europe, and Germany in particular. Often made from cereals, potatoes and the residue of sugar beet, Schnapps closely resembles vodka, but the traditional name has been retained in order to underline its authenticity.

GASTSTÄTTE AND *GASTHAUSBRAUEREI*

Anyone interested in beer will be well advised make an effort to visit a *Gasthausbrauerei* or *Gaststätte*. These are inns that brew their own beer. Typically German and widespread throughout the country, they provide an opportunity to discover wonderful-tasting beers. They also offer typical Berlin dishes such as *Eisbein* (see p.28).

Gaststätte
Glasowerstraße 27, Neukölln
☎ 626 88 80

Open every day from 9am. Situated in one of the oldest parts of Berlin, this brewery is known for its tasty Rix beer and traditional cuisine.

Gasthaus Bräuerei Aschinger
Kurfürstendamm, 25
☎ 882 55 58
Open every day from 8.30am.

The oldest brewery in Berlin (1892), that's also renowned for its incredibly light lager.

AN INTRODUCTION TO BEER

Besides the breweries, there are other places in Berlin where connoisseurs, beer-lovers and the uninitiated alike can discover the delights of beer and find out more about it.

Mommsen-Eck Haus der 100 Biere
Mommsenstaße, 45
☎ 324 25 80
Open every day from 8am.
This 'house of a hundred

beers' has something to satisfy even the most curious visitor, with the most expensive beer in the world (DM16 for 33cl), the most exotic beer (made from bananas) and beer all the way from Tasmania.

QUICK GUIDE TO BEER DRINKING

Bier vom Fass/Hahn: draught beer
Flaschenbier: bottled beer
Pilsner: first brewed by the Czechs, Pilsener – which takes its name from the Czech city of Pilsen – is the most commonly drunk and best-loved beer made from hops in Germany
Weizenbier: a typically Bavarian wheat beer
Beck's: imported from northern Germany, this certainly isn't the lightest and most sparkling of ordinary German beers, but it's the most widespread in Berlin
Prost/Prosit!: Cheers!

Berliner Bier Fakultät
Strausberger Platz, 1
☎ 24 72 04 54
Open every day from 11am, Sat.-Sun. 10am.
Founded by leading specialists, this faculty is a friendly place where you can come to exchange opinions and discover the history and the various types of beer.

KNEIPE AND BIERGARTEN

The Berlin beer, *Molle* (is drunk in a *Kneipe* in winter and in a *Biergarten* in summer. A *Kneipe* is a kind of bistrot that serves refreshments and a *Biergarten* is an open-air café often shaded by trees where you can sit at a large table and sip beer and nibble *Schrippen*, *Buletten* or an assortment of charcuterie (*Wurstplatte*).

A CITY OF MUSEUMS

After reunification, Berlin found itself the proud owner of around 180 museums, some of which were doubles – one in the East, one in the West. Before integrating this formidable heritage, the city must restore and reclassify the works dispersed during the war. Until 2001, it also will be carrying out a vast restructuring of its national museums around three centres in particular – Dahlem, the Kulturforum and Museuminsel.

MUSEUMINSEL

Now reintegrated into West Berlin, the Museuminsel (Museum Island), was considerably impoverished by the war and the division of Germany. From 2001 onwards, it should recover a good part of its ancient and archeological riches. The Altes Museum will display its entire collection of Classical and Greco-Roman antiquities. The Alte National-galerie, which is closed until 2001, will regain its 19th-century masterpieces and enrich its collection with the collection of Egyptian art, which has been on display at Charlottenburg and its superb collection of ancient sculptures (from Dahlem) and paintings by Italian and Dutch masters. It will also once again display one of the most important medal and coin rooms in Europe. Lastly, the partially-ruined Neues Museum, which won't see the light of day until 2005, will receive the other part of the collection of Egyptian art, as well as the departments of pre- and proto-history, all of which are currently housed at Charlottenburg.

Portrait of Friedrich II by Zisemis

View of the Parade Ground by Rosenberg

paintings from the Romantic gallery of Charlottenburg castle. The Bodemuseum will recover its famous bust of Nefertiti after it has been cleaned, as well as part of its

DAHLEM, A CENTRE OF NON-EUROPEAN ART

For several years, this series of museums in the former West Berlin has undergone great change, beginning with the transfer to the Kulturforum of its famous picture gallery. Partly closed for cleaning and the reorganisation of the collections, the museums of Dahlem will devote their space to ethnology and house collections from the Pacific regions, as well as Africa and Asia. It will not be until after the departure of the picture gallery and the imminent transfer of the collections of Islamic art and ancient sculptures, that the Museum of Ethnology will have enough space for its immense reserves.

KULTURFORUM, ANCIENT AND MODERN EUROPEAN ARTS

The Kulturforum (Culture Forum), in the neighbourhood of the Wall, will be the

One of the rooms in the Brücke Museum

alter ego of West Berlin's Museuminsel. The plans made since 1989 to remedy the museums' lack of space have finally been realised. The highlight of this Forum is the famous picture gallery, a collection of works of art once divided between East and West Berlin, which, since 1998, has been reassembled. The rich Museum of Applied Arts and the Prints Room complete this remarkable collection of 13th- to 18th-century European paintings. The nearby Neue Nationalgalerie continues artistic reflection in the 20th century.

CITY MUSEUMS AND OTHER COLLECTIONS

In spite of their scope and world renown, the big national museums aren't the only ones worthy of a visit. Berlin offers a quantity of other smaller museums that are equally fascinating. These include the Bröhan-Museum for fans of Art Deco and Jugendstil, the Berggruen collection, based on the works of Picasso, and the Brücke Museum, with its remarkable German Expressionist paintings. The German Technology Museum, with its full-size planes and trains, and the Natural History Museum, with some of the biggest dinosaur skeletons in the world, are both worth a visit. The Stasi Museum (State Police), which recently opened on the original site of the organisation, is far more disturbing.

A YOUNG CONTEMPORARY ART SCENE

To this diversity of museums and exhibitions can be added the dynamism of a brand-new generation of contemporary art galleries that are open to German and international trends (see notes at back of guide). Their development was accompanied, in 1996, by the establishment of an important annual contemporary art fair. To keep up momentum, a first biennial art fair saw the light of day in 1998. These events went hand in hand with the political will to develop the contemporary art scene, which was expressed by the opening of a large museum designed to house art from the sixties to the present day, the Hamburger Bahnhof (Invaliedenstraße, 50-51).

THE ALTERNATIVE SCENE

Over the years, the alternative movement, born in Berlin in the late 1970s, has marked the cultural and political landscape of the city. A hothouse of new ideas, it gave birth to an extremely lively underground culture that still attracts young people, artists and antiestablishment protesters, who come to Berlin to find a new way of life.

THE BIRTH OF THE ALTERNATIVE MOVEMENT

In 1968, students in West Berlin became the driving force behind the protest movement. After violent confrontations with the police, many students realised they couldn't spark off world revolution by themselves. If there was to be a revolution, it had to come about by changing attitudes and everyday reality. A good number of them left university to set up small self-run communities, often in unoccupied houses, whose aim was to live and to think differently. The alternative movement was born.

THE SQUATS

While the first occupied houses (*besetzte Häuser*) appeared in the mid 1970s, the real wave of occupation didn't take place until 1979. At that time there was a serious housing shortage crisis in Berlin and many owners were allowing their vacant buildings to become dilapidated in order to benefit from generous government grants that would eventually allow them to build brand new housing. Outraged by their attitude, young people decided to take possession of the vacant houses. Unfortunately, the situation

led to violent clashes between owners and squatters. In order to ease the tension, the State offered the squatters legal contracts. As the movement gradually became legal, a second wave of occupation occurred just after the fall of the Wall. The most revolutionary squatters, who refused any form of compromise with the State, took advantage of the general confusion to seize a large number of empty houses in East Berlin. They were followed by a new generation of young people, most of whom came from the south of Germany. From the centre, the movement spread out to Prenzlauer Berg, Friedrichshain and Lichtenberg. While some communities still cling almost ferociously to their independence, most of the occupied houses, like those in Prenzlauer Berg, are well integrated into society and have become part of the Berlin landscape.

THE EAST BERLIN UNDERGROUND SCENE

Despite the GDR's authoritarian regime, small alternative protest groups formed in East Berlin.

Although these groups were no longer forced underground, they were nevertheless very active and often had to display great inventiveness in escaping the ever-present control of the Stasi (State Police). Prenzlauer Berg, which would later be compared to its western counterpart, Kreuzberg, became the centre of the alternative movement in the eighties, with the first communities of squatters, alternative cafés, gay bars and independent groups of artists. The full extent of the movement in East Berlin only became apparent after reunification.

A WAY OF LIFE

Over the years, what was originally a minority movement peculiar to Berlin, pervaded the entire cultural and political life of Germany. Thanks to the 'alternative' movement, many local mutual aid and environmental awareness associations were set up. Cafés, organic product cooperatives, self-run craft centres and a new, original and unofficial form

THE MAIN ALTERNATIVE CENTRES OF BERLIN

UFA-Fabrik
Viktoriastraße, 13, Tempelhof.
A small self-run society with around sixty residents that boasts a theatre, cinemas, a renowned organic bakery and a circus school.

Mehringhof
Greisenaustraße, 20, Kreuzberg.
The former factory has become quite a business, with a bookshop, cycle shop and its very own bank.

Tacheles
Oranienburgerstraße, 58-56, Mitte.
The best-known of all the alternative art centres of the old East. It boasts a café, a cinema, a number of workshops and a theatre.

of culture exemplified by the 'off' theatres (see p. 14) also made its appearance. Perhaps the most telling example of the movements success is the leftist newspaper, the *Taz* (the *TAgesZeitung*). Founded in 1979 as a reaction against the *Springer* conservative press group, it's now sold throughout Germany. The movement has also given birth to a powerful political party, the Alternative Liste (A.L.) ecology party, which, since 1992, has joined forces with the famous Green Party, *die Grünen*.

TECHNO AND THE LOVE PARADE

The musical phenomenon of the nineties, techno music, was partly born in Berlin, a city open since the 1970s to electronic music and the underground movements. It was on the record decks of the German capital that the best-known American DJs mixed new synthetic sounds in the early nineties. Once the music of reunification, techno has since become an extremely popular musical movement. The success of the Love Parade is proof of this.

UNDERGROUND MOVEMENT

After the fall of the Wall, the east revealed itself as an ideal, if unexpected, setting for techno music. The deserted buildings, such as former bunkers, hangars, administrative offices and areas formerly occupied by the Stasi (State Police), were dream locations to set up illegal clubs or organise giant clandestine rave parties at which thousands of techno fans could come together. This shift of the techno scene from west to east meant that many West Berliners encountered the east for the first time.

THE FIRST CLUBS

Among the many more or less ephemeral clubs to open in the early eighties, Le Tresor is definitely the most legendary and one of the few to last. This former bank dating from the 1920s, located in the cellars of a department store, soon became the best-known underground venue of the international techno scene. It was here that the most prominent DJs of Detroit, Chicago and Berlin mixed their music.

In their day, Le Tresor, Le Bunker and L'E-Werk (a former electricity generating station) were the most important places on the Berlin techno scene.

LOVE PARADE

With the Love Parade, techno music left the underground, illegal setting of the clubs and rave parties and went out onto the streets. The original idea for the event came from the legendary DJ Dr Motte, who wanted to give the music a new dimension along the lines of the Rio de Janeiro carnival and the big American parades. The first Love Parade, on the theme of *Love, Peace and Unity*, took place shortly before the fall of the Wall. Only a hundred and fifty people took part in the event, along with three vans on which the DJs mixed music non-stop.

Six years later, nearly half a million people crowded the streets to dance to the sound of techno. In 1998, over a million people paraded through the heart of Berlin, from the Victory Column to the Ku'damm. What was once a small, unpretentious parade has now become a huge event sponsored by large companies and supported by the German Senate.

unofficial form of communication imported from the United States appeared – the flyer. This was a card showing the date and location of the next party. At first circulated informally and covertly, flyers are now widely distributed in record and clothes shops, clubs and cafés. Besides passing on information, they also marked the beginning of a brand new graphic culture specific to the techno movement. The other widely-used means of communication is the magazine. In Berlin, one of the first and best-known was called *Frontpage*. This magazine not only provided information about the music scene and forthcoming events, but also included

FRONTPAGE AND *FLYER*

Alongside the techno movement, a new,

TECHNO FASHION

Fashion is an essential part of the techno movement. Seventies fashion, war, natural catastrophes, science-fiction and cartoon heroes have all been sources of inspiration. The important thing is to be at odds with the norm and average, every-day fashion. With the fall of communism and the withdrawal of allied troops, the Berlin flea markets were flooded with military accessories and uniforms until as late as 1993. These became a major source of inspiration for the Berlin techno scene. Russian army shirts, flying goggles, American fatigues and old Adidas waistcoats from the eighties became essential clothes and accessories. In Berlin today, army surplus is still a popular favourite among techno music fans and others.

a number of articles on clothes fashion and the latest trends. More than just a magazine, *Frontpage,* with its constantly changing layout, became a vehicle for a whole new lifestyle. While it is no longer in production, others, such as the little booklet called, quite simply, *Flyer*, have taken over and are just as popular.

BERLIN, A CITY IN THE COUNTRY

Despite being the capital, Berlin is a city of water and greenery, which you'll notice immediately upon your arrival by car or plane. Berlin is like an island surrounded by lakes and forests. But the water and greenery aren't confined to the outskirts of the city, they also form part of its inner landscape, beginning with the Tiergarten, the huge park in the very centre of Berlin, and the River Spree, which flows through the city from one side to the other. In spring, you'll be struck by the wide, tree-lined avenues, the countless squares and the vast, leafy municipal parks. With so many oases of greenery, Berlin has all the appearance of a provincial town.

THE TIERGARTEN, A FOREST IN THE CITY CENTRE

Situated in the very heart of the city, the Tiergarten is the most famous and best-loved park in Berlin. The city's 'green lung', as it is known by Berliners, made its appearance in 1650 in the form of an enclosed wildlife reserve designed as a hunting ground – hence the name 'animal garden'. It wasn't until the 19th century that it was landscaped as a park by one of the most important and active landscape gardeners in Berlin, Peter Joseph Lenné. Winding paths, walks, lawns, flower gardens, small lakes and ponds all help to make this vast domesticated 225ha/ 556 acre forest a delightful place in which to relax.

A ZOO NEAR THE KU'DAMM

The zoo (*Zoologischer Garten*), which is the continuation of the Tiergarten, is a vast expanse of greenery designed for walking and entertainment. The oldest zoo in Germany, it opened in 1844 and has the largest number of animal species in the world (around 1,200 species). The giant aquarium, with its alligators,

and the aviary, with its large, colourful birds, are are both particularly fascinating. With an original layout by Lenné, the zoo is a haven of peace just a stone's throw from the great boulevards of the Kurfürstendamm (see p. 51).

THE BOTANICAL GARDEN

The botanical garden (*Botanischer Garten*) is an oasis of greenery in the south of Berlin, not far from the famous museums of Dahlem. Since 1897, plants from all over the world have been displayed and studied here. In addition to its scientific side, the garden is remarkable

for the elegant layout of its gardens and the amazing variety of plants, trees and flowers that it contains. Its numerous greenhouses – the most impressive of which is a 25m/82ft high glass palace – make it equally pleasant to visit in summer and winter. Entrance, Unter den Eichen, S-Bahn Botanischer Garten and U-Bahn Dahlem-Dorf. Open every day Nov.–Feb. 9am–4pm, Mar.–Oct. 9am–5pm, Apr.–Sep. 9am–8pm. Museum open Tue.–Sun. 10am–5pm.

THE *SCHLOSSPARK*

Berlin has several royal parks, the most famous of which is undoubtedly the park of the Charlottenburg castle (*Schlosspark*). Designed to harmonise with the architecture of the castle by the French landscape gardener, Siméon Godeau in 1687, it was the first Baroque garden in Germany. In the early 19th century the strict geometry of the Baroque garden was softened with the introduction of an English-style garden, designed by Lenné. The setting of the park and castle on the banks of the river Spree favoured access by water. Today, the castle bridge (*Schlossbrücke*) is still one of the main departure points for boat trips in Berlin.

TRIPS ON THE WATERWAYS

Besides the Spree, Berlin has a number of canals, including the Landwehrkanal, in the south of the city. This network of waterways offers one of the

most beautiful and most interesting trips to the heart of Berlin. Departing from Charlottenburg castle bridge, the boat passes through the heart of the future government district, enters historic Berlin at the Museuminsel, continues its course in the direction of alternative Kreuzberg and then turns towards one of the loveliest parts of Berlin, the willow-lined Landwehrkanal, with its many footbridges.

VIKTORIA MUNICIPAL PARK

In addition to the royal parks and gardens, Berlin boasts a great number of big municipal parks. There isn't a single part of the city that doesn't have its own park with its regulars. In Kreuzberg, the Viktoriapark is possibly

one of the most popular in the western part of Berlin. Designed round a waterfall by the architect Schinkel, this romantic park offers a marvellous view of the district and its surrounding area. The 22m/72ft high Gothic steeple that can be seen at the top of the waterfall gave its name to the district called 'cross mountain' (see pp. 54-55).

THE MUNICIPAL PARKS OF THE EAST

In the east of Berlin, there are no fewer than fourteen big municipal parks, including the Friedrichshain Volkspark. Designed by Lenné in 1848 and later enlarged by his pupil Gustave Meyer, the park was intended to be the counterpart of the Tiergarten for the working-class districts in the east of the city. After 1945, it was redesigned around the debris of the Wehrmacht bunkers, which explains the presence of the two grass and tree-covered mounds with spiral paths winding their way to the top. Further south, the Treptower is the park that has most retained its East

German character. This is the site of the imposing Soviet memorial *(Soujetisches Ehrenmal)*, erected to the memory of the 5,000 soldiers of the Red Army. The colossal size of the statues and the layout of the site are highly impressive. Its location on the banks of the Spree makes it the departure point for many of the cruises run by the *Weiße Flotte* company

(for further information, go to the Treptower Park S-Bahn station).

THE CEMETERIES

The cemeteries of Berlin – of which there are very many – are havens of peace and greenery that are pleasant to visit in summer. In addition to their mysterious romantic charm, they have a special place in the German memory. The Friedhof

der Dorotheenstädtischen in Chausseestraße (open every day 8am–8pm), is the Highgate of Berlin. In the Städtischer Zentralfriedhof Friedrichsfelde in Gudrunstraße lie the principal protagonists of German socialism, including the radical Rosa Luxemburg (open every day 7.30am–dusk). Finally, the Jüdischer Friedhof, at Weissensee, is a poignant reminder of the size of Berlin's Jewish community before the second World War (Sun.–Thu. 8am–5pm, Fri. 8am–3pm).

THE MÜGGELSEE

The city has a wealth of waterways. In addition to a

multitude of smaller lakes, it has three very sizeable ones – the Tegelsee in the north, the Wannsee in the south, and the Müggelsee in the south-east. Wherever the location, these lakes are easily-accessible and very popular with swimmers and wind-surfers in summer. In winter, their frozen surfaces attract ice skaters. The Müggelsee is by far the largest of these; situated in the middle of a large expanse of woodland, it has a fully-equipped beach and was a popular holiday resort with East Berliners before reunification. From the Müggelturm, in the Müggelsee forest, you can enjoy a panoramic view of Berlin and the lake from a height of 115m/377ft.

THE WANNSEE

The Wannsee, in the west, is famous for its long, sandy beach, which first opened in 1907. Its boardwalks and beach huts, reminiscent of the 1930s, give it an old-fashioned air which, along with its practical amenities, makes it very popular with Berliners. Besides being a prominent holiday resort, Wannsee is also notorious for the conference that determined the fate of the Jews on 20 January 1941,

which took place in the villa at no. 58 (Haus der Wannsee Konferenz, Am Grossen Wannsee, 56-58, Tue.–Fri. 10am–6pm, Sat.–Sun. 2–6pm, free entry). On another note, one of the most picturesque places in Berlin, the Pfaueninsel (Peacock Island) is in the middle of the lake. The small mock-ruined castle that can be glimpsed on the island was built in 1794 in accordance with the wishes and plans of Friedrich-Wilhelm II.

THE VAST FOREST OF GRUNEWALD

To the north of the Wannsee, lies the Grunewald, the most exensive forest in Berlin. With its evergreen and deciduous trees, it's an ideal place for excursions. Along shady paths in the north of the forest lies the city's foremost residential district, with its small, neo-Gothic castles, affluent-looking houses and Rococo residences built for dignitaries of the state. This is also the site of one of the most luxurious hotels in Berlin, the *Schlosshotel*. In the north-west of the forest stands a red-brick neo-Gothic tower, the Grunewaldturm, which offers a panoramic view of the city of Berlin and the River Havel as far as Potsdam.

BERLIN CUISINE

It has to be said that, apart from a few typical products and certain local dishes, Berlin isn't exactly renowned for its gastronomy. Perhaps to remedy this lack, the city has long since opened its gates to foreign cuisines. This trend, which has become more marked since reunification, reveals the multicultural and cosmopolitan nature of a changing city. With both chic and traditional restaurants and oriental and international cuisine, there's something to suit all tastes and budgets.

TRADITIONAL BERLIN CUISINE

Berlin cuisine is simple, filling and cheap. More often than not, it consists only of a main course,

which almost always includes meat (usually sausages or pork) accompanied by salad, red cabbage, sauerkraut and boiled potatoes.

Among these meat-based dishes, the *Eisbein mit Sauerkraut und Erbspüree* is undoubtedly the best. It consists of a knuckle of salt pork, served with sauerkraut and pease pudding that's really delicious when cooked in the traditional way and is especially recommended on cold winter days. The other typical dish is *Bulette*, which is also known as *Frikadelle*. This owes its name to the Huguenot community that settled in the city around the end of the 18th century. The dish consists of minced meat mixed with white bread, onions and spices, which is then shaped into balls, which are cooked and eaten cold, sometimes with *Senf* (slightly sweet German mustard).

SPREEWALD CUCUMBER

The cucumber *(Gurke)* of the Spree forest *(Spreewald)* is undoubtedly the most widely-grown fruit of the region. Preserved in a number of ways (more often than not bottled), it can be found in a wide variety of guises. The *Saure Gurke* is certainly the most popular variety. Rediscovered after reunification, this large

gherkin preserved in vinegar has formed part of the Berlin culinary heritage since the 1920s. Beelitz asparagus is a real seasonal event in Berlin. When the first asparagus appears (between April and early June) Berliners are in the habit of inviting their friends to a *Spargelessen* (asparagus dinner) and all the restaurants in the city have asparagus-based dishes on their menus. Besides the *Gurken* and the Beelitz asparagus, the black radishes of the Spreewald *(Meerettich)*, the turnips of Teltow *(Rübchen)* and, of course, the inevitable Brandenburg potatoes *(Kartoffeln)* have once again become the flavours of the day since reunification.

fish once again feature on the restaurant menus. The famous recipes of the *Land* include such delicacies as pike with diced bacon *(Hechtspeck)* or Spreewald sauce *(in spreewälder Sauce)*, eel with herbs in sauce *(Aal Grün)* or white beer *(in Weissbier)* and flambéed medallion of hare *(Hase-Medaillon flambiert)*.

GAME AND FISH

With its many lakes, rivers and forests, the city of Berlin, or rather the *Land* of Brandenburg, offers a wide choice of game and fish. Specialities include wild boar

ROLLS AND *PFANNKUCHEN*

Berlin has little in the way of typical pastries or bread. Among the countless German rolls, only the *Schusterjunge* (with rye) and the *Knüppl* (with wheat and milk) are said to come from Berlin, not to mention the very popular *Schrippe,* which

(Wildschwein), roe deer *(Reh)*, hare *(Hase)*, carp *(Karpfe)*, pike *(Hecht)*, tench *(Schleie)* and, above all, eel *(Aal)*, which is fished in large quantities. Having almost disappeared under the GDR regime, game and is none other than the traditional roll. It's a sign of the times that some baker's shops in the former East Berlin have been making their own version of *Schrippe* again over the last

few years. More compact and unleavened, these are known as *Ostschrippen*. In terms of pastries, *Pfannkuchen* is undoubtedly the most popular cake. It's a large jam-filled doughnut that's mainly eaten on New Year's Eve and at Carnival time. Strangely enough, the doughnut, which is known as *Pfannkuchen* in Berlin, is called a *Berliner* throughout the rest of Germany.

FRÜHSTÜCK IN BERLIN

The word *Frühstück*, means 'breakfast' in English but can be considered the German equivalent of brunch. It's the high point of the weekend. Generally eaten at around 10 o'clock in the morning, it can last until late in the afternoon (4 or 5pm) in certain *Kneipen*. In Berlin, it's something of an institution. Almost all the cafés or *Kneipen* offer a vast array of à la carte *Frühstück*.

These can be oriental in origin or based on smoked fish, charcuterie or cheese. *Bauernfrühstück* (country breakfast) with potato omelette, is probably the most filling. The *Frühstücksbuffets* (breakfast buffet) offered by some *Kneipen* at the weekend in particular is still the most convivial.

NOUVELLE CUISINE

While the fall of the Berlin Wall allowed the city to

broaden its range of food, it also upset traditional eating habits. Over the last few years a new, far less substantial and more refined form of cuisine has made its appearance. This so-called 'nouvelle cuisine', which is often international in style, is characterised by a choice of simple but varied foods, perfectly cooked and above all, presented in an attractive, original, if not to say meticulous, way. The appearance and popularity of this type of cuisine in Berlin gave rise to a whole new generation of chic, trendy Italian restaurants serving dishes such as artichokes with truffles as well as the more traditional *frutti di mare*.

CURRYWURST, A HOT SAUSAGE

More often than not, Berlin cuisine is first and foremost a quick snack you grab at lunchtime or any other time of day, propped up at one of the many

district, its popularity spread within a few years to the rest of the city, to such an extent that it competed with *Curry-wurst*. Lighter and easier to digest than its equivalent elsewhere in Europe, the Berlin *doner* consists of slices of mutton grilled

stands known as *Imbisse*. The best-known of these snacks is a *Currywurst*. This consists of a grilled sausage smothered in ketchup and sprinkled with curry powder, and is generally eaten with a chunk of bread (*Brot*) or a portion of chips (*Pommes frites*). It first appeared in Berlin after the war and fast became popular as the Berliners' national dish.

THE *DONER KEBAB*

The *doner kebab* was imported into West Berlin by Turkish immigrant workers in the early 1970s. Originally limited to the Kreuzberg

on a vertical spit, together with onion rings, sliced tomato, a little salad, red cabbage and garlic and chilli sauce, all served in lightly-toasted Turkish bread. A Lebanese version of this cheap and delicious meal consists of marinated meat, vegetables and salad. This is often less substantial and more delicate in flavour. *Chicken doner*, which is of course made from chicken, is another recent variation on the theme.

MEALTIMES

There's nothing to worry about as far as mealtimes are concerned. Whether you like going to bed late or getting up early, there'll always be somewhere open for you to get a bite to eat. Apart from the large restaurants (where it's

essential to book), most eating places are open round the clock, so you won't have any difficulty finding a café where you can have breakfast at midday. In the same way, if you want to have lunch at 4 o'clock in the afternoon, there are many *Kneipen* that will accommodate you. Given the special intensity of Berlin nightlife, some places happily go on serving after midnight and many *Imbisse* are open for 24 hours a day.

THE *IMBISS*

The *Imbiss* is to Berlin what the takeaway is to London. It consists of a cabin, van or small restaurant at whose counter you can have a quick bite to eat. Open until late at night, these little refreshment stands are one of the best reflections of the city's multicultural character. Besides the well-known and popular *doner kebab* and *Currywurst* you can find *falafels*, minipizzas, Turkish pizzas and, in the Vietnamese *Imbisse*, *China Pfanne* (fried Chinese noodles).

The Biggest Building Site in Europe

Since the fall of the Wall, the urban landscape of the German capital has undergone an unprecedented transformation. With building sites populated by cranes, streets criss-crossed by countless pipes and buildings hidden behind scaffolding, everything about the city is changing. The most striking aspect of this transformation can be seen in the giant building projects. The Potsdamer Platz, the government district, the central station and the embassies are all grandiose projects that have been entrusted to famous architects, whose work never ceases to amaze.

Potsdamer Platz

Having been taken over by Daimler-Benz, Sony and ABB in the early 1990s, Potsdamer Platz has in a few years become one of the biggest building sites in Europe. Gigantic machinery and land dug to a depth of 100m/yds below ground level have helped to make the square a major tourist attraction. In five short years, what was once a vast no-man's-land has become a veritable city. Restaurants, hotels, a shopping centre, a 3D cinema, offices, a media library, a cinema school and museums are now the main attractions of the new centre, which was inaugurated in October 1998. Since then, Potsdamer Platz seems to have returned to its former role as one of the liveliest squares in Europe.

The Government District

Between the Tiergarten park and the bend in the river Spree the future Parliament and government district is taking shape. Designed by the Berlin architect Alex Schultes, the project aims to make a complete break with history and tradition. Original, elegant buildings will stretch from east to west in a band 1½ kilometres/ 1 mile long, along which the public will be able to stroll. Currently closed, the district will open its gates in 2005. North-east of this band, not far from the Brandenburg Gate, stands the Reichstag, henceforth known as the Deutscher Bundestag. The controversial restoration of this building, which was burnt down by the Nazis, was entrusted to the English architect, Sir Norman Foster. After many disagreements with the Senate, the architect finally agreed to renovate the former dome, but as a place in which visitors would be able to visit and explore.

THE TUNNEL UNDER THE SPREE

While the Parliament and government buildings reach skywards, an unusual system of tunnels is being dug under the city. High-speed trains, the U-Bahn and cars, too, will soon pass under Potsdamer Platz, the Tiergarten park, the government district and the Spree. This incredible operation, undertaken to develop a relatively little-used north-south route through the city, has been an enormous project. Among other things, it has meant digging in sandy ground

OPEN PIPEWORK

The many pink, blue and purple pipes that you see about you are a characteristic feature of a city being rebuilt. They first appeared in the early nineties to drain away waste water and have since become an integral part of the urban landscape.

and changing the course and levels of the Spree in order not to interrupt maritime traffic during the building works.

THE NEW CENTRAL STATION

To complete this system of tunnels, a new central station, situated not far from the former Lehrter station, should see the light of day in

INFO BOX

Inside this intriguing red box mounted on piles, you'll find full information on the progress of all the major building projects in the form of exhibitions, animated films and models. The building, which has been installed in the vicinity of Potsdamer Platz since 1995, is due for removal at the end of 2000.

2003. Conceived an as immense glass and steel cathedral by the Hamburg architect Gerkan Marg, it's destined to become one of the biggest stations in Europe. In addition to the traditional east-west route, the station will also serve the north-south route and will play a decisive role in the European transport network.

THE EMBASSIES OF PARISER PLATZ

With the moving of the government from Bonn to Berlin, the city has had to build new foreign embassies. Among these are the embassies of the former allies, the British, American and French. The three embassies, which were destroyed during the Second

World War, are to be rebuilt on their former sites around the Pariser Platz. The only drawback to the plan is that the sheer size of some of the buildings means that the Brandenburg Gate is in serious danger of being dwarfed!

Berlin Practicalities

GETTING ABOUT

Don't be fooled – though Berlin may seem provincial, it actually covers a vast srrawling area (see maps on pp. 80–85). Make good use of public transport – it's a great way to get about the city. Besides being huge, Berlin possesses a considerable number of museums, monuments and curiosities. You won't be able to visit the whole city in two or three days. Don't despair, just see how you feel and visit the places that appeal to you most. These may include a lake, a building site and a collection of Ancient Egyptian artefacts or a piece of the Wall, a castle and one of the 'in' districts, by way of contrast.

BY U-BAHN, TRAM AND BUS

Berlin has the best public transport system in Germany, with the U-Bahn (underground), S-Bahn (underground express), buses and trams (in the eastern part of the city) running from 4am to 12.30am (1.20am in the case of the S-Bahn). Night owls are catered for by a network of night buses marked with the letter 'N'.

At the weekend, the U9 and U15 U-Bahn lines run all night. A ticket costing DM3.90 is valid for any means of transport and allows you to travel for two hours in all the AB zones of the city. For short journeys (three U-Bahn stations or six bus or tram stops), there are DM2.50 tickets called *Kurzstrecke*. You can buy your ticket from bus drivers, the ticket machines in U and S-Bahn stations, or on trams. Don't forget to validate your ticket in the red boxes on U and S-Bahn station platforms and in trams and buses. If you need to use public transport all day long, buy a *Tageskarte* (one-day card), which is practical and economical (DM7.80 for zones A and B and DM8.50 for zones A, B and C, which takes you as far as Potsdam). The *WelcomeCard* (DM29) is ideal for families and allows an adult accompanied by one to three children under 14 years of age to travel for three days within the A, B and C zones of the UBB network. The card also entitles you to reductions for museums and theatres, and for coach tours of Potsdam as well as Berlin. You can buy *WelcomeCards* at tourist information offices and hotels. For visitors who are staying a little longer, a *Wochenkarte* (weekly card) costing DM40 is probably the best bet.

It's worth bearing in mind that a trip on the S-Bahn from Zoologischer Garten to Alexanderplatz, a journey on the U2 and U15 overhead U-Bahn lines or a ride on the famous 100 bus (see p. 47) can be an excellent way to get to know the city and its monuments.

BY BIKE

If the weather is fine, the ideal way to see the city is by bike. Bicycles rule the streets of Berlin and the many cycle paths, marked by a red stripe on the ground, are scrupulously respected by car drivers. If you're on foot, beware of walking on a cycle path, or you'll probably get hooted at or, worse still, crashed into. Outside the rush hour, bikes are allowed in the central coaches of the U and S-Bahn. You just have to buy an extra ticket.

To hire a bike, call **Bike City ☎ 28 30 48 48** (central reservations) or go along to: Rosenthalerstraße, 40–41, in the Hackeschen Höfen (Mitte) open Mon.-Fri. 10am-7pm, Sat. 10am-4pm. Augustraße, 29 (Mitte) Mon.-Fri. 10am-7pm, Sat. 10am-3pm. Bergmannstraße, 9 (Kreuzberg) Mon.-Fri. 10am-7pm, Sat. 10am-3pm.

BY TAXI

There are plenty of taxis about which can be recognised by their signs and their yellowish-cream colour. They take up to three people and are relatively easy to flag down. Rides cost DM4 for a pick-up, plus DM2.30 per km/⁵/₈ mile in the daytime and DM2.40 at night (11pm-6am). Many drivers take credit cards. For a 5-minute ride or one of less than 2km/1¹/₄ miles, ask for a *Kurzstrecken* (short journey), which will cost only DM5. If you call a taxi by phone, you have to add DM2 to the cost of the ride.

Spree Funk
☎ 44 33 22
Funk Taxi
☎ 26 10 26
Taxi Funk
☎ 690 22.

BY TAXI-BIKE

Over the last couple of years, a new, unconventional means of transport, the rickshaw, or taxi-bike, has appeared on the streets of Berlin. Generally driven by students, this original, eco-friendly means of transport has been a great success.

Velotaxi GmbH Berlin
☎ 44 35 89 90.

MAKING A PHONE CALL

In the space of a few years, the old yellow phone boxes have all been replaced by pink and grey DT (Deutsche Telekom) boxes. With a few exceptions, these take DM12 and 50 phone cards, which you can buy at post offices or newspaper stands. Some phone boxes take credit cards. The few coin boxes still in existence are mostly to be found in cafés. Calls are cheaper after 6pm, at the weekend and on public holidays. If you phone from your hotel room, it will cost you three or four times as much as a normal call. To call a Berlin number from within the city, dial the number only without the 030 code. You only need this for calls outside the city.

For calls to the UK from Berlin, dial 00 44 (followed by the number you're calling), to Ireland, dial 00 353, to Australia, dial 00 61, to New Zealand, dial 00 64 and to the USA and Canada,

dial 001. For calls to Berlin from abroad, dial the international dialing code followed by 4930.

SENDING POSTCARDS AND LETTERS

You can only buy stamps in post offices, which are open 8am-8pm on weekdays and 9am-noon or 1pm on

Saturdays. A 20g letter costs DM1.10. To send postcards or letters, post them in the *Andere Postleitzahl* slot of the yellow letterboxes.

CHANGING MONEY

Berlin banks have different opening times according to whether you're in the east or the west of the city. They're usually open 9am-3.30pm on Mondays and Wednesdays and 9am-6pm on Tuesdays and Thursdays, and sometimes close as early as 12.30pm on Fridays. Generally speaking, it's unusual to find a bank open on a Saturday (for further information, see p. 9).

GUIDED TOURS

In Berlin, four big companies have the monopoly of guided tours of the city, especially by bus. They generally offer similar tours at identical prices. A grand tour of Berlin costs DM39, a short tour DM30 and an excursion to Postdam DM59. Further details can be obtained from tourist information offices. Themed tours, such as 'Berlin before the fall of the Wall' and 'Literary Berlin' are of far greater interest. With commentaries in either German or English, these are guaranteed to take you off the beaten track. You'll find details of the tours in the magazines and flyers available from tourist information offices. If you come to Berlin between April and September, be sure to take a boat ride along the canals and on the Spree. It's a very restful way to spend three hours seeing old Berlin, as well as unusual industrial and urban areas.

Bruno Winkler
☎ 349 95 95.

City Schiffahrt H. G. Gabriel
☎ 345 77 83, **F** 345 99 33.
The cruise specialists. A complete tour, *Spreekrone*, costs DM22-24.

OPENING TIMES

The current reorganisation of Berlin museums won't be complete until the end of

A BIRD'S-EYE VIEW OF BERLIN

If you've got a good head for heights, you can get an interesting and unusual view of Berlin from a helicopter. Departing from Tempelhof Airport, a ride over the city costs around DM200 per person.
Kanzler
☎ 694 94 90
F 694 93 01.

2000. To avoid disappointment, it's best to check in advance that those you want to visit are open to the public. The same is true of monuments, which are generally closed on Monday. The vast majority of tourist attractions are open 10am-6pm Tuesday to Friday and 10am-5pm on Saturday. There are quite a few public holidays in Germany –the most significant in Berlin being 3 October, German Reunification Day. Phone in advance to make sure the places you want to visit aren't closed. With the exception of Marian, Nikolai and Sophienkirche, most churches are closed outside of services. If you have a card entitling you to a reduction, don't forget to bring it with you.

TOURIST INFORMATION OFFICES

Here you'll find plans of the city, flyers and full details of Berlin's cultural life. You'll also be able to reserve your hotel rooms (for a DM5 commission) and theatre or concert seats. For DM3.50, the bilingual German/English magazine *Berlín* will give you up-to-the-minute information on all the latest events.

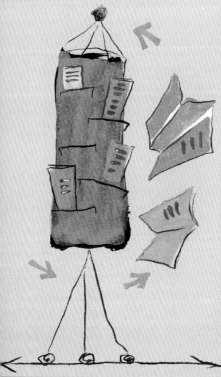

USEFUL NUMBERS

Police ☎ 110

Emergencies ☎ 31 00 31

Information ☎ 011 88

Lost property:
Found by the police:
Zentrales Fundbüro,
Platz der Luftbrücke,
(Tempelhof) ☎ 69 95
Found on public transport:
BVG Fundbüro
Frauenhoferstraße 33-36,
(Charlottenburg)
☎ 25 62 30 40.

Internet Cafés
Internet Café Haitaick
Brunnhildestraße 8
Schöneberg 12159
☎ 85 96 14 13
Train: S4/U9 Bundesplatz

Internet Café Alpha
Dunckerstraße 72
Prenzlauer Berg 10437
☎ 447 90 67
Train: U2 Eberswalderstraße

German Directory Enquiries: ☎ 118 33

International Directory Enquiries: ☎ 118 34

Europa-Center
Budapesterstraße 45,
Charlottenburg
S and U Zoologischergarten
Mon.-Sat. 8am-10pm,
Sun. 9am-9pm.

Brandenburg Gate
Pariser Platz, south wing of the gate
Every day 9.30am-6pm.

Information and reservations
Hotline : 00 49 30/25 00 25
🆓 00 49 30/25 00 24 24
E-mail: information@btm.de
or reservation@btm.de
Internet: www.berlin.de.

Around Alexanderplatz

in the footsteps of history

Overlooked by the *Fernsehturm* (Television Tower) and made famous in Alfred Döblin's novel *Berlin Alexanderplatz*, the 'Alex' has seen the ups and downs of history. Visited by Czar Alexander I when he came to Berlin to seal the alliance with Prussia, scene of revolutionary clashes and city and shopping centre of the former East Berlin, the square lies in the eastern part of medieval Berlin. You may be intrigued by the mix of architectual styles – but they all had a political purpose.

❶ Volksbühne★★

Rosa-Luxemburg-Platz
☎ 247 76 94.

Founded in the late 19th century, the Association of Popular Theatre advocated open access to culture. Housed in this building nicknamed 'the battleship' since 1914, it has always been one of the most innovative theatres in the city. Since 1992, the magical productions of Erwin Piscator have given way to the creativity of Frank Castorf. Venture into the left wing for drum 'n' bass (Monday), tango (Wednesday) or salsa (Tuesday) in the *Roter Salon*.

❷ Karl-Marx-Allee★★

Designed by Hermann Henselmann and previously known as Stalinallee, this street is 2.5km/1½ miles

long and 90m/295ft wide, and has borne witness to a political regime that did not go unchallenged. In June 1953, the building workers went on strike, protesting at conditions, but the uprising quickly met with brutal repression, as Soviet tanks were sent in to restore order.

❸ Nikolaiviertel★★

First recorded in 1264, the medieval heart of the twin towns of Cölln and Berlin earned its living by trade and fishing. Destroyed and rebuilt over the centuries before finally being rebuilt in 1987, it has an old-fashioned air, as if time had stood still here. The 13-16th century Nikolaikirche (church of St Nicolas), houses an exhibition of the city's early

centuries under its brightly-painted intersecting ribs. The Rococo Ephraim Palace opposite is a reminder of the banker's influence in the reign of Friedrich II.

❹ Fernsehturm★
Daily, May-Oct. 9am-1pm, Nov.-Apr. 10am-midnight. Entry charge.

The pride of its designer (Henselmann), the 365m/ 1,200ft high Television Tower was built in the 1960s. It's a nuisance on sunny days when a cross, known as the 'pope's revenge' by many Berliners, is reflected across the city. The view is worth the trip, though you may have to queue. Otherwise, it's the kingdom of kitsch, with a revolving restaurant for tourists at the top and a complex of cafés and exhibition halls at the foot.

❺ Marienkirche★
Rathausplatz
Mon.-Thu. 10am-4pm, Sat.-Sun. noon-4pm.

Dwarfed by the Fernsehturm and opposite the Rotes Rathaus (red town hall) (1869), this simple church is the last vestige of the city's medieval village origins. You'll leave entranced by the *Totentanz* (1485), a frieze depicting the dance of death, discovered in 1860.

❻ Märkisches Museum★
Am Köllnischen Park 5
Tue.-Sun. 10am-6pm
Entry charge.

Although this building may appear Gothic, it was designed to complement several Brandenburg monuments. Inside, the history of the city is told, from prehistory to the present day, marked by its many Slav influences, to which the beautiful 11th-century silver jewellery bears witness. Outside, you may take pity on the lonely bears in the bear pit. Then head for the Märkisches Ufer. The Spree then comes into view, lined

with Classical buildings. The Ermeler Haus, at nos. 10-12, is the setting for paintings by Georg Baselitz.

❼ ZUR LETZTEN INSTANZ★
Waisenstraße, 14
☎ 242 55 28
Daily, noon-1am.

Tucked away in a little street forgotten by time, you'll find this restaurant serving traditional cuisine. The menu, peppered with legal expressions, offers 'Zur letzten Instanz' (as a last resort) a knuckle of ham *(Eisbein)* of proverbial taste and dimensions that must be washed down with a *Berliner Weiße*.

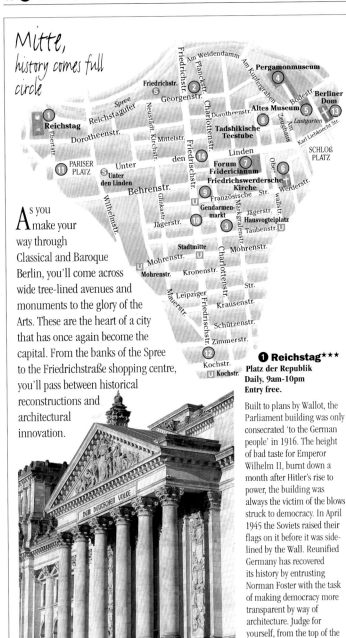

Mitte, history comes full circle

Pergamonmuseum ④

Friedrichstr. ②

Friedrichstr. ⑤

Altes Museum ⑧

Bodestr.

Berliner Dom ⑬

Tadshikische Teestube

Reichstag ①

Unter ⑭ den Linden

Linden

Forum Fridericianum ⑦

⑥

Friedrichswerdersche Kirche

⑨

PARISER PLATZ ⑪

Gendarmenmarkt

⑩

③ Hausvogteiplatz

Stadtmitte

⑫

A s you make your way through Classical and Baroque Berlin, you'll come across wide tree-lined avenues and monuments to the glory of the Arts. These are the heart of a city that has once again become the capital. From the banks of the Spree to the Friedrichstraße shopping centre, you'll pass between historical reconstructions and architectural innovation.

❶ Reichstag★★★
Platz der Republik
Daily, 9am-10pm
Entry free.

Built to plans by Wallot, the Parliament building was only consecrated 'to the German people' in 1916. The height of bad taste for Emperor Wilhelm II, burnt down a month after Hitler's rise to power, the building was always the victim of the blows struck to democracy. In April 1945 the Soviets raised their flags on it before it was side-lined by the Wall. Reunified Germany has recovered its history by entrusting Norman Foster with the task of making democracy more transparent by way of architecture. Judge for yourself, from the top of the dome, whether the enterprise has met with success.

❷ Berliner Antik- und Flohmarkt
Georgenstraße, 191-195
☎ 204 43 01
Tue.-Sun. 11am-6pm.

Under the arcades of the S-Bahn, a series of shops exhibits curios and Art Nouveau furniture. A great place to come for a browse. Watch out for such items as solid silver candle-holders (DM1,500) or a 1920s coffee service. If tableware isn't your thing, then let yourself be captivated by the jewellery and let it transport you back to the era of Chaplin, or rather Fritz Lang.

❸ Gendarmenmarkt
★★★

This is probably the most homogeneous architectural group in the city. Many Huguenots settled here after the Edict of Nantes was revoked in 1685, forcing them to flee to Protestant countries. The Französischer Dom and the Deutscher Dom bear witness to their enforced exile. Built to satisfy the French and Prussian reformed faiths, these two churches form a harmonious balance with the Schauspielhaus, a renowned concert hall, home to the Berlin Symphony Orchestra.

❹ Pergamonmuseum
★★★

Bodesstraße, 1-3
Museuminsel
☎ 20 90 55 55
Tue.-Sun. 10am-6pm,
Thu. 10am-8pm
Entry charge.

Modelled on the Acropolis as a refuge for the arts, the Museuminsel embodies a century of Prussian cultural politics. Colonnades, capitals and statues adorn a succession of neo-Classical buildings. A bridge over the Spree gives access to the most impressive of these.

Built to house the altar of Pergamon (160 BC), the Babylonian gate of Ishtar (600 BC) and other ancient architectural treasures, the museum creates *in situ* a journey of initiation into historical monuments.

❺ Altes Museum★★
Am Lustgarten
☎ 20 90 55 77
Tue.-Sun. 10am-6pm
Entry charge.

You reach the oldest museum in Germany through the Lustgarten, ('pleasure garden'). Now restored to its original function, the park was for a long time the scene of military parades of every kind for which the severity of the colonnade made a particularly fitting backdrop. Inaugurated in 1830, Schinkel's work is, however, most impressive, with a dome that seems to defy the laws of physics. In spite of the restoration work in hand, it's possible to gain access to a selection of paintings.

❻ Friedrichs-werdersche Kirche★★
Schinkelmuseum
Werderstraße
☎ 20 90 55 55
Tue.-Sun. 10am-6pm
Entry charge.

Every Berliner worthy of the name harbours a respectful admiration for the architect and sculptor Schinkel. Heavily influenced by Classical styles, some consider him to be the first contemporary designer. The elegant purity of this neo-Gothic church conceals a museum devoted to the delicate works of the master and his no less illustrious colleague, Schadow.

❼ Forum Fridericianum★★
Unter den Linden/Bebelplatz.

The cultural and artistic centre of the Prussian monarchy, the Forum combines the Staatsoper, Berlin's first theatre designed by Knobelsdorff, the Alte Bibliothek, a former royal library, Humboldt University and Sankt-Hedwigs-Kathedrale. But history often surfaces where it's least expected in Berlin. In the Bebelplatz, the unusual 'Empty Library' bears witness to the book burning of May 1933, while inside the Neue Wache, the Pietà by Käthe Kollwitz pays homage to the victims of state violence.

❽ Tadshikische Teestube★★
Am Festungsgraben Palace
☎ 204 11 12
Mon.-Fri. 5pm-midnight, Sat.- Sun. 3pm-midnight.

From the outside there's nothing to suggest that you'll be transported to the steppes of Asia once you've crossed the threshold of this former home of the artists of the GDR. Allow yourself time to learn about the formal ceremony that accompanies the preparation of Russian tea, brightened up in this instance with vodka and jam. Sitting cross-legged and lulled by oriental vapours, you won't be far from the silk road. There are plenty of snacks to accompany all of this.

❾ Borchardt★★
Französischestraße, 47
☎ 20 38 71 17
Every day 11.30-1am.

A blend of French and Italian cuisine awaits you in this famous old rest-aurant, considered by some to be one of the best in Berlin. It's frequented by the Berlin of the fashion, business and political worlds, who flock here to eat at the elegant tables under tall pink marble pillars. The spacious interior has the atmosphere of a smart brasserie. If it's fine, choose a table in the inner courtyard.

❿ Friedrichstraße★★

Where a shady crowd gathered before the war, attracted by the nightlife, there are now only businessmen and big brand names. From the glass building of the Galeries Lafayette to the light squares of District 206, architects from all over the world have left their mark here. Further proof awaits you in the nearby Schützenstraße, where the Milanese architect Aldo Rossi has mixed Baroque and neo-Renaiss-ance styles.

⓫ Pariser Platz★★

Closed to the west by the Brandenburg Gate, the Pariser Platz is making every effort to return to its pre-war symmetry. In one corner, the Adlon Hotel has been rebuilt, a close replica of its former glory, it's an exceptionally grand old hotel which was once the epitome of class and luxury. The Brandenburg Gate, which dominates in the square, has deep historical significance to Berliners. Topped by the famous *quadriga* (horse-drawn chariot), it was originally built as a triumphal arch in 1791 and was to become a rallying place for the Nazis and later a symbol of the division of Germany. These

days the square itself is full of stalls selling communist souvenirs to tourists.

⓬ Checkpoint Charlie★

If you want to look for traces of the Wall, Checkpoint Charlie seems the obvious place to start. Only the Café Adler remains as a reminder of the spot where the tanks of

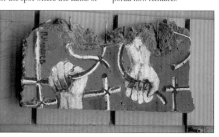

the two blocs confronted each other in a stand-off in 1961. In its memory, artist Frank Thiel has placed monumental portraits of an American and a Russian soldier here. Anyone keen on history should visit the Museum Haus am Checkpoint Charlie.

⓭ Berliner Dom★
Am Lustgarten
☎ **20 26 91 33**
Mon.-Sat. 9am-8pm, Sun. noon-8pm. Entry charge.

Altered many times, destroyed and later rebuilt in accordance with the wishes of Emperor Wilhelm II, this centre of Prussian Protestantism must once have been impressive. It now stands alone, but should be pictured against the backdrop of the Hohenzollerns' castle. The building altered by Schlüter at the end of the 17th century was blown up by the GDR in 1950, and only the portal now remains.

⓮ UNTER DEN LINDEN★★

Of the old bridle path linking the castle to the Tiergarten, only the rustic echo of the name 'under the lime trees' remains. When Berlin acceded to the status of a royal residence, the monarchs hastened to give it the *via triumphalis* it was lacking. Headed by the Brandenburg Gate, along its 400m/yds lie symbols of Prussia's cultural and military influence – the opera house, the royal library, the university and the Arsenal, soon to be turned into a museum of German history by Ieoh Ming Pei. As you make your way up the avenue, pause on the *Schlossbrücke* by Schinkel, which is made entirely of Carrara marble and granite.

Around Potsdamer Platz

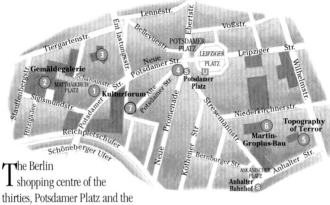

The Berlin shopping centre of the thirties, Potsdamer Platz and the surrounding area, was left in ruins after the war. The black market flourished in the neighbourhood of the former centres of Nazi power, before the Wall turned it all into a no-man's-land. Now that it's the geographical centre of the city once more, the district is seeking a new reputation as a cultural centre, just a stone's throw from the future Shoah memorial.

city by creating an island of culture that would be the counterpoint of the Museum-insel. Designed by Mies van der Rohe, the Neue Nationale-galerie is striking for the purity of its lines. The esplanade is a museum crossroads giving access to the Kunstgewerbe-museum (Museum of Applied Arts) and Kupferstichkabinett (Prints Room). Take time to stop and admire the sculptures by Calder and Moore.

❶ Kulturforum★★★
Potsdamer Platz.

Also known as the Tiergarten complex, the Cultural Forum has taken thirty years to complete. The idea was simple: to oppose the division of the

❷ Gemäldegalerie ★★★

Matthäikirchplatz, 8
☎ 266 21 00
Tue.-Fri. 10am-6pm,
Sat.-Sun. 11am-6pm
Entry charge.

Picture Gallery
Kulturforum

Inaugurated in 1998, the museum houses the sumptuous collections of Dahlem and the Kaiser-Friedrich-Museum, which had been separated since 1939. The exhibits are displayed around wells of natural light and six centuries of European art can be seen in this way. In view of the wealth of paintings housed here, it's better to concentrate on a particular period or country.

3 THE PHILARMONIE
Herbert-von-Karajan Straße, 1
☎ 25 48 80
Mon.-Fri. 3-6pm,
Sat.-Sun. 11am-2pm.

Some say its yellow outline resembles a big top, but no-one remains indifferent to the extraordinary acoustics of this octagonal concert hall, designed by Hans Sharoun. The music and architecture are so much in harmony that it's a pleasure to both ears and eyes. Under its conductors Arthur Nikisch, Herbert von Karajan and Claudio Abbado, the Berlin Philharmonic Orchestra has always enjoyed an international reputation. There are frequent concerts and you may be lucky enough to get last-minute tickets on the evening from the *Abendkasse* (6pm).

4 Potsdamer Platz★★

Built at enormous cost, the new business, games and multimedia centre is gradually becoming an essential stop on the way from the east to the west of the city. Renzo

Piano, who designed the Pompidou Centre in Paris, is the architect responsible for much of the regeneration scheme which incorporates luxury hotels, a casino and a multiplex attract a crowd of curious onlookers.

5 Topography of Terror★★
Stresemannstraße, 110
☎ 25 48 67 03
Daily, 10am-6pm
Entry free.

The area between Wilhelm-Straße and Prinz-Albrecht-Straße bears the scars of a century of German history. At the heart of the former Nazi ministerial district, above the cells of the Gestapo and bordered by the remains of the wall, the museum-monument by the Swiss architect Peter Zumthor is set to be made permanent. Meanwhile, there is a display of archive photos.

6 Martin-Gropius Bau★★
Stresemannstraße, 110
☎ 25 48 60
Tue.-Sun. 10am-8pm
Entry free.

The former Museum of the Applied Arts is one of the few buildings to have survived the allied bombardments. The building, which is testimony to the architectural know-how of two of Schinkel's young pupils, was restored with a view to housing museums and temporary exhibitions. A frosted glass roof over the atrium floods the neo-Classical square with light.

7 Tizian★
Grand Hyatt
Marlene-Dietrich-Platz, 2
☎ 25 53 12 34
Daily, 9-1am.

To give yourself a break from the endless human tide, take a few quiet moments of self-indulgence and experience the hotel architecture of the third millennium with a long coffee break. Sobriety, clarity and serenity are they keywords of this space. Take in the dramatic, futuristic architecture – it's out of this world.

Tiergarten, the green heart of the city

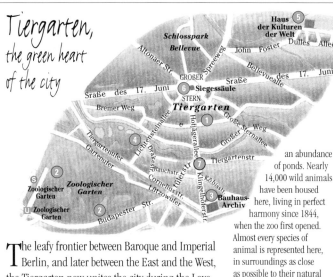

The leafy frontier between Baroque and Imperial Berlin, and later between the East and the West, the Tiergarten now unites the city during the Love Parade. Named in honour of the workers revolt of East Berlin (1953), the broad avenue Straße des 17 Juni offers a unique view of the Brandenburg Gate. In the West, the architectural exhibition of 1957 gave rise to the Hansaviertel, which is marked by the designs of Aalto, Le Corbusier and Gropius.

an abundance of ponds. Nearly 14,000 wild animals have been housed here, living in perfect harmony since 1844, when the zoo first opened. Almost every species of animal is represented here, in surroundings as close as possible to their natural habitat. The nearby aquarium (combined tickets available) is also well worth a visit.

❶ Tiergarten★★★

Once a wild hunting reserve filled with deer, the 'animal garden' was turned into a pleasure park by order of Friedrich II and it's now an oasis of greenery in the centre of the city. In part wild and dense, the 220ha/544 acre park takes on the air of an English garden round the Bellevue Palace. While there's a memorial to the revolutionary leader Rosa Luxemburg on the banks of the Landwehrkanal, no trace remains of the sandy desert left by the park's destruction in World War II.

❷ Zoologischer Garten★★

Hardenbergplatz, 8
☎ **25 40 10 or**
☎ **212 77 06 (aquarium)**
Daily, 9am-6.30pm
Entry charge.

Originally the royal pheasant farm founded in the 18th century, the zoo is set in a wooded park with

❸ Bauhaus Archiv★★

Klingelhöferstraße, 14
☎ **25 40 02 78**
Wed.-Mon. 10am-5pm
Entry free on Mon.

The Bauhaus school of architecture and art founded in Weimar in 1919 by Gropius was forced to move several times, to Dessau and then to Berlin, ending in its closure by the Nazis in 1933. Declaring that the purpose of the Bauhaus was to realise 'the unity of art and technology', Gropius strove to bring about

collaboration between engineers and artists. Designed by the master himself, this museum bears witness to his decisive influence on the Berlin style. As well as designer objects, architects' plans, functional furniture there are works by Kandinsky and Klee.

❹ Café am Neuen See★★
Lichtensteinallee, 2
☎ 254 49 30
In summer daily,
10am-11pm,
in winter Sun.
10am-8pm.

After drifting dreamily along in a boat, you'll be glad to get back to some good Bavarian fare at this café on the banks of the Neuer See, a delightful group of lakes in the Tiergarten. If you don't fancy a *Bretzel* or *Leberkäse*, there are also giant pizzas just waiting to be tasted. Students converge here, along with others taking a breather and some respite from the city's hustle and bustle on the banks of the shady lake.

❺ Haus der Kulturen der Welt★★
John-Fuster-Dulles-Allee, 10
☎ 39 78 71 75
Entry charge.

Nicknamed 'the oyster' by Berliners, this former conference centre was the

architectural bombshell of the 1957 exhibition. The concrete roof, rebuilt after it collapsed in 1980, curves effortlessly complemented by Moore's 'butterfly' sculpture, which hovers above the surface of the water. Home to world cultures since 1989, it's a venue for exhibitions, theatrical performances and, above all, concerts and dance performances.

❻ Siegessäule★
Mon. 1-6pm,
Tue.-Sun. 9am-6pm
Entry charge.

Immortalised on screen by Wim Wenders in *Wings of*

Desire, the Victory that stands on top of the column celebrates Prussia's military victories over the Danish, Austrian and French armies. Originally (1873) placed in front of the Reichstag, the monument was moved to the heart of the Tiergarten, in accordance with the wishes of the Nazi architect Albert Speer. Once you've climbed the 70m/230ft column, you'll find the outstanding view worth all the effort.

❼ 100 BUS★★
The stop outside the zoo.

The 'Hunderter' bus has become an institution. Besides linking the east and the west of the city at breakneck speed, it also has the bonus of taking you through the Tiergarten from one side to the other. From the Zoo station, you pass the Bellevue Palace. Then you enter the brand-new government district, before passing through the Brandenburg Gate in the direction of Alexanderplatz.

Charlottenburg,
from the palace to the museums

The palace built by the Hohenzollerns, which bears the name of the first queen of Prussia, was badly damaged in World War II. Now faithfully rebuilt and surrounded by cultural centres, it lies at the heart of the district where the artist Heinrich Zille caught the likeness of the Berlin people in his sketches, at the beginning of the 20th century.

kings of Prussia. It was in this home of enlightened despotism that the philosopher Leibniz was received, and Friedrich II, who was a patron of the arts, housed his collection of paintings by Watteau here. From the Porcelain Room to the Romantic Gallery, everyone will find something of interest in the many sumptuous rooms open to the public.

❶ Charlottenburger Schloss★★★
Luisenplatz
☎ 320 911
Tue.-Fri. 9am-5pm,
Sat.-Sun. 10am-5pm
Entry charge.

Built by the prince-elector Friedrich I as a summer residence for his wife, the palace was progressively enlarged in the 18th century modelled on the Palace of Versailles, to show the increasing power of the

❷ Ägyptisches Museum★★★
Schloßstraße, 70
☎ 20 90 55 55
Tue.-Fri. 10am-6pm,
Thu. 10am-8pm,
Sat.-Sun. 11am-6pm.
Entry charge.

You really must visit this museum – if only to be captivated by the enigmatic smile of the bust of Nefertiti, the museum's most treasured exhibit. This collection, the fruit of many 19th-century German archeological digs in Egypt, joined that of the Museuminsel at the start of the 21st century. Meanwhile, the Coptic sarcophagi and ebony and granite statues merit special attention.

❸ Schlossgarten★★
Entry free.

The park is an inviting place for a country outing and is popular for Sunday walks. From the Baroque garden stretching in front of the main body of the palace you quickly move on to a more rustic landscape bathed by ponds, criss-crossed by little wooden bridges and bordering on the Spree. As you walk along, look out for the Belvedere, which is hidden in the greenery. This Baroque pavillion, designed by Carl Gotthard Langhans, houses a precious collection of

porcelain made in the royal factory. When you return to the palace, pause for a moment in front of the peaceful mausoleum to admire the statue of Queen Louise by the sculptor Christian Daniel Rauch.

❹ BERGGRUEN COLLECTION★★
Schlossstraße, 1
☎ 326 95 80
Tue.-Fri. 10am-6pm,
Sat.-Sun. 11am-6pm
Entry charge.

Born in Berlin in 1914, Heinz Berggruen emigrated to the United States in 1936 where he became a famous collector and art dealer. A friend of Picasso, his wealth of acquisitions is now available to the public. A large collection of around sixty works by Picasso, among them *The Yellow Pullover* and *Still Life with a Blue Guitar*, hang side by side with paintings by Klee, Braque, Matisse, Van Gogh and others.

❺ Bröhan-Museum★★
Schlossstraße, 1a
☎ 321 40 29
Tue.-Sun. 10am-6pm
Entry charge.

The museum owes its existence to Karl H. Bröhan's love of Art Nouveau and

Art Deco. On the occasion of his 60th birthday, he gave his collection to the city of Berlin. From the glassware by Emile Gallé to the furniture by Hector Guimard, Peter Behrens and Louis Majorelle, the whole of the ground floor is arranged in rooms dedicated to their designs. This shouldn't distract your attention from the gold and silverware, porcelain and paintings of the German and Scandinavian Jugendstil though.

❻ Villa Oppenheim★
Schloßstraße, 55
☎ 34 30 41 51
Tue.-Thu. 11am-5pm,
Fri. 11am-3pm,
Sun. 3-6pm
Entry free.

With its neo-Classical villas (no. 67) and its leafy aspect, the Schlossstraße exudes a feeling of fin-de-siècle romanticism. To prolong this feeling, call in at no. 55, a villa that has been turned into a cultural centre. Painters and sculptors exhibit their works here, while writers read out their prose and you'll be able to have a cultural discussion over a cup of coffee.

Charlottenburg, the chic Ku'damm

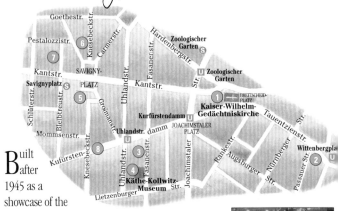

Goethestr.
Pestalozzistr. ⑥
⑦
Kantstr.
Savignyplatz ⓢ
SAVIGNY-
PLATZ
⑤
Kneseckstr.
Carmerstr.
Uhlandstr.
Fasanenstr.
Kantstr.
Hardenbergstr.
Zoologischer
Garten ⓢ
Zoologischer
Garten ⓤ
BREITSCHEID-
PLATZ
① Kaiser-Wilhelm-
Gedächtniskirche
Schlüterstr.
Bleibtreustr.
Grolmanstr.
Mommsenstr.
Uhlandstr.
Kurfürstendamm
JOACHIMSTALER
PLATZ
Tauentzienstr.

ᴮuilt ᴬfter 1945 as a showcase of the

Kneseckstr.
Kufürsten-str.
⑧
Uhlandstr. ⓤ
③
④
Fasanenstr.
Uhlandstr. damm
Joachimstaler Str.
Rankestr.
Augsburger Str.
Nürnberger Str.
Wittenbergpla
②ⓤ
Passauer Str.
Käthe-Kollwitz-
Museum
Lietzenburger Str.

free world, Charlottenburg has the artistic tradition of the twenties behind it. From Otto Dix to Max Reinhardt, writers and painters have met in the literary cafés of the Ku'damm. Quieter since reunification, the district is still a pleasant place in which to stroll. From the shady streets round Savignyplatz to the shops of Fasanenstraße, you're surrounded by the Berlin of yesteryear.

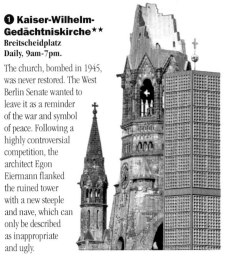

❶ Kaiser-Wilhelm-
Gedächtniskirche★★
Breitscheidplatz
Daily, 9am-7pm.

The church, bombed in 1945, was never restored. The West Berlin Senate wanted to leave it as a reminder of the war and symbol of peace. Following a highly controversial competition, the architect Egon Eiermann flanked the ruined tower with a new steeple and nave, which can only be described as inappropriate and ugly.

❷ KaDeWe★★
Tauentzienstraße, 21-24
☎ 21 21 0
Mon.-Fri. 9am-8pm,
Sat. 9am-4pm.

The *Kaufhaus des Westens* (KaDeWe) is to Berlin what Harrods is to London. Opened in 1906 and enlarged many times, it prides itself on containing the grocery department in Europe. Literally stormed by East Berliners after the fall of the Wall, it offers such an abundance of merchandise that it's easy to understand the dazed expressions of some of the people at the time.

❸ Literaturhaus★★

Fasanenstraße, 23
☎ 882 65 52
Daily, 9.30-1am.

Feel like a country outing in the middle of the city? Then stop off at this haven of peace and tranquillity. This villa, surrounded by a large garden, houses a Viennese-style café-restaurant. Novelists and poets come here regularly to read their works, and you can always find a copy of them in the bookshop tucked away on the ground floor. At teatime, order the best *Apfelstrudel* in Berlin.

❹ Käthe-Kollwitz Museum★★

Fasanenstraße, 24
☎ 882 52 10
Mon., Wed.-Sun. 11am-6pm
Entry charge.

The works of artist Käthe Kollwitz, which come from the private collection of Hans Pels-Leudsen, are displayed on the four floors of this turn-of-the-century residence. It's a choice setting for the woman whose artistic creativity was fed on the daily observation of the working-class families of Prenzlauer Berg at the time of the Great Depression.

❺ Bücherbogen★★

Savignyplatz
☎ 312 19 32
Mon.-Fri. 10am-8pm, Sat. 10am-4pm.

Nestling under the arcades of the S-Bahn, this bookshop which specialises in art, architecture and design has an impressive stock. Whether you're looking for the works of a Scandinavian designer or a précis of New York architecture, there's plenty of interest for you to discover. Many English editions are available.

❻ Florian★★

Grolmanstraße, 52
☎ 313 91 84
Daily, 6pm-3am.

This restaurant located between fashion and antique shops and café terraces is frequented by journalists and actors. It's true that people come here to be seen, but as the chef and his menu keep up their standards, eating here is also a pleasure. Try the *Nürnberger*

Rostbratwürstchen auf Kraut (small grilled sausages with cabbage).

❼ Fiebelkorn, Kuckuck, Langhein★

Bleibtreustraße, 4
☎ 312 33 73
Mon.-Fri. 11am-7pm, Sat. 11am-4pm.

Three young designers exhibit their creations here, with their studio at the back. They all have their own styles and work with different fabrics at reasonable prices (DM200-300). The first designer concentrates on wedding dresses. The second prefers designs of coloured pleats, which are very glamorous for the evening. Last but not least, the third seems to have a predilection for simple cuts in silk and linen.

❽ THE KURFÜRSTENDAMM ★★

The construction of this avenue, which was personally defended by Bismarck, began in 1886. The buildings with their richly-sculpted façades and the width of the road combined to make it the counterpart, if not the rival, of Unter den Linden. This shopping street, better known as the Ku'damm, is now home to the big names of fashion.

The alternative Kreuzberg of Oranienstraße

The legendary district of eighties West Berlin, where illegal occupations and autonomous communities once flourished, Kreuzberg has retained its artists' workshops and antiestablishment character. As you walk down Oranienstraße, you'll enjoy the exotic aromas wafting from the Turkish community's many shops. As you come to the banks of the Landwehrkanal, the famed air from an operetta by Paul Lincke that summons up the bracing qualities of the Berliner Luft may come to mind: 'Das ist die Berliner Luft, Luft, Luft ...'

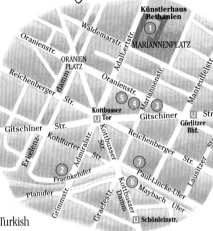

❶ Künstlerhaus Bethanien★★
Mariannenplatz, 1-3
☎ 25 88 41 41
Mon.-Fri. 10am-7pm
Entry charge.

The back of beyond when the Wall formed its barrier, this place is still off the beaten track. A former hospital, it was the site of illegal occupations in the 1970s. Saved from certain destruction, the building has now been given a new lease of life by setting it up as an art centre. From the former chapel, now converted into a gallery for young artists, to the garden, which is turned into an open air cinema in the summer (the programme starts at 9.45pm), all forms of artistic expression are represented here.

❷ Fraenkelufer★
Dug in the mid-nineteenth century, the Landwehrkanal, an inland waterway, runs through an area like little piece of Amsterdam, which is a pleasant place to stroll before *Frühstück* (breakfast). Don't hesitate to venture beyond the glass façades and fanciful balconies of nos. 44 and 38. You'll discover a fine example of contemporary urbanism designed by Inken and Heinrich Baller for the international architecture exhibition of 1987.

❹ HANFHAUS★★
Oranienstraße, 192
☎ 614 81 02
Mon.-Fri. 11am-7pm,
Sat. 11am-4pm.

The hemp house is impossible to miss. Decorated with huge cannabis flowers, it's certainly eye-catching. All kinds of weird and wonderful products await you here – hemp beer, chocolate and cake as well as clothes and cosmetics. If you feel like exporting a few grains, be careful – not everywhere is as tolerant as Berlin.

❸ Amrit★★
Oranienstraße, 202
☎ 612 55 50
Daily, 11-1am.

A delightful Indian restaurant that's taken over every evening by a young clientele for whom the modestly-priced dishes (DM15) and generous helpings are an irresistible lure. Everything is arranged so that you'll get to know your fellow diners better over the tandoori chicken served on a smoking grill. While you're about it, don't forget to order a *patura*, the toasted bread that takes the edge off the spices.

❺ SO 36★
Oranienstraße, 20
☎ 615 26 01
Concerts from 9pm.

To distinguish the alternative Kreuzberg from the other parts of the district, some nostalgic people still use the old postcode (36), which indicates its geographical position (in the south-west).

This centre of alternative rock and symbol of the punk generation has regular gay and lesbian nights that are anything but restrained.

❻ Ankerklause★
Maybachufer/
Kottbusser Damm
☎ 693 56 49
Daily, from 10am
(except Mon. 4pm).

This bar resembling an old-fashioned café and dance hall, has become the haunt of young people looking for a good night out. Overlooking the Landwehrkanal, it's an ideal place from which to cast an

eye over the tourist-laden boats that sail up and down. If you think you can detect a whiff of the orient on Tuesdays and Thursdays, it's because a Turkish market has set up shop on the left bank of the canal.

❼ Anne Malderle★
Paul-Linke Ufer, 44
☎ 61 28 58 85
Mon.-Fri. 11am-8pm,
Sat. 11am-4pm.

Nestling between the crowded terraces of the *Café am Ufer* and the *Cucina Mediterranea*, Anne Malderle's shop has a minimalist air. The designer makes classic dresses, three-quarter-length coats and tops with pure lines in three main colours – black, grey and white. The watchword of the house is simplicity and sobriety.

Around Kreuzberg, a touch of the Mediterranean

Watered and divided by the Landwehrkanal, Kreuzberg is a patchwork of cultures. Lacking real architectural unity, the western part of the district is nevertheless marked by the *Mietskasernen* (high-rise flats), a succession of inner courtyards built at the height of the city's population explosion by the Berlin architect James Hobrecht. However, not a trace of Prussian severity remains. Bohemian craftsmen, artists and students have long reigned supreme.

Map labels: Jüdisches Museum, Franz Klühs Str., Friedrichstr., Lindenstr., Wilhelmstr., MEHRINGPLATZ, Hallesches Ufer, Hallesch. Tor, U, Obentrautstr., Mehringdamm, BLÜCHER-PLATZ, Blücherstr., Hornstr., Großbeerenstr., Mehringdamm, Baruther Str., Zossener Str., Yorckstr., Riehmers Hofgarten, St.-Bonifatius Kirche, Gneisenaustr., Gneisenaustr., Schleiermacherstr., Katzbachstr., Kreuzbergstr., Bergmannstr., MARHEINEKE-PLATZ, Viktoriapark, Meffiesselstr., Mehringdamm, CHAMISSO-PLATZ, Fidicinstr., Friesen Str.

❶ Jüdisches Museum ★★★
Lindenstraße, 9-14
☎ 28 39 74 44
Guided tours Sat.-Sun. by appointment.
Entry charge.

The challenge to be met when showing the influence that Berlin Jews had on the political, economic and cultural life of their city was in representing their absence. The clever deconstruction of the Star of David by American architect of Polish origin, Daniel Libeskind, is awe inspiring. The cold metal and sharp lines of the new Jewish Museum are a vivid reminder of a tragic history. The emotive display of the war years (temporarily housed in the Martin-Gropius-

Bau, see p. 45) is due to be moved here in the autumn of 2000, in the mean time the tour of the building itself is certain to leave you moved.

❷ Riehmers Hofgarten ★★
Yorckstraße, 83-86.

This neo-Renaissance architectural group will take you back to the turn of the 20th century. The mannered façades, colonnaded balconies and friezes are all suggestive of gracious living. However, alongside all this, the church of Sankt Bonifatius (1907) is tightly surrounded by blocks of flats, to ensure every inch of space is used.

❸ Viktoriapark ★★
The first impression you get of this leafy park clinging to the slope of a hill in Kreuzberg, is that of an endless waterfall

As you stand on one of the bridges that span it, you expect to see salmon leaping, yet in 1821, this was no more than a bare hill, until this park was created to commemorate the 'wars of liberation' against Napoleon. The monument crowned with a cross (*Kreuz*) has given its name to the district.

4 Bergmannstraße★

Connecting Viktoriapark to Marheinekeplatz, this street is the answer to the shopper's prayer. Stroll along among the Turkish and Arab fruit, vegetable and spice stalls and let yourself be tempted by a *falafel* or *doner kebab*. Among the objects on sale at no. 105, you're sure to find something unique. A little further on, look out for the unusual glass shutters of the café at no. 103. If its terrace is full, *Barcomi's* (no. 21) offers delicious brownies and legendary muffins.

5 Junctionbar★★
Gneisenaustraße, 18
☎ 694 66 02
Daily, 8pm-5am.

On two floors, one dedicated to the bar, the other to the music scene, this renowned jazz cellar also stages soul and funk. With its young clientele,

the Junctionbar reflects a district inhabited by quantities of artists and those who prefer alternative lifestyles. If you feel like partying until dawn, a DJ takes over from the musicians after their set.

6 Osteria n°1★
Kreuzbergstraße, 71
☎ 786 91 62
Daily, noon-1am.

In Berlin, a little touch of the south is always welcome. The hidden back garden of this Italian restaurant in the shadow of Viktoriapark is

definitely the place to come. Whether you choose pizza, tagliatelle or antipasti, the important thing is to enjoy to the full this haven of peace surrounded by greenery.

7 Chamissoplatz★

The sloping streets you encounter on your way to Chamissoplatz are a reminder of Prussian rigour. Now restored and painted, the façades of the houses bear witness to the gentrification of a district abandoned after the war. For further proof of this, go along to the Haifischbar, Arndtstraße, 25, where you can share sushi and cocktails with the trendy local population.

---

8 RADIO ART★★
Zossener Straße, 2
☎ 693 94 35
Tue.-Fri. 1-6pm,
Sat. 10am-1pm.

Even if you're not a collector, a wireless freak or a television addict, this museum, where you can buy anything or have anything repaired, is still worth a visit. You'll find the most cumbersome of valve radios and early televisions displayed side by side with very unusual portable transistor radios.

Spandauer Vorstadt, the light and shade of the city

This former working-class suburb grew up along the fortifications north of the historic centre in the 18th century. Neglected at the time of the GDR, the district is once more coming to life behind the dilapidated façades and narrow courtyards of the high-rise flats. Designers and artists in search of new territory are taking over the labyrinth of streets round the fashionable cafés. This is the heart of the new Berlin – come and take its pulse.

❶ Neue Synagoge and Centrum Judaïcum★★★

Oranienburger Straße, 28-30
☎ 28 40 13 16

Sun.-Thu. 10am-6pm,
Fri. 10am-2pm
Entry free.

Both the symbol and emblem of a vanished Berlin, the golden dome of the largest synagogue in Germany crowns a building with a troubled past. Designed by Eduard Knoblauch and inaugurated in 1866, was damaged but not destroyed on *Kristallnacht* thanks to a warning given by a policeman. Severely damaged by bombing in 1943, however, restoration did not begin until 1988 and today houses a museum, information centre and temporary exhibitions about Jewish culture.

❷ Tacheles★★★

Oranienburger Straße, 54-56
☎ 28 26 185.

In a street full of bars, this half-ruined building comes as somewhat of a surprise. Only the walls remain of the pre-war shopping arcade and technological exhibition hall, from where the first television broadcast in the world was transmitted. In 1990 a group of young artists known as the *Tacheles* occupied the building and since then the collective have exhibited monumental sculptures here, as well as rganising concerts, exhibitions and experimental film shows. At first sight, it all seems a bit confusing, but once you've explored the various levels and conquered the maze, the café *Zapata* will be ideal for a relaxing drink.

9 Sophienkirche★★
Große Hamburger Straße, 9-31
Sun. 10am-1pm, Wed. 3-6pm, Sat. 3-5pm.

Thanks to Queen Sophie-Louise, third wife of Friedrich I, this was the first Protestant parish church to be built in the district (1712). Flanked by blocks of flats since the early 20th century, the Baroque bell-tower overlooks a shady cemetery where the famous historian Leopold von Ranke is buried.

4 Alter Jüdische Friedhof★★
Große Hamburger Straße, 26
Entry free.

What today appears to be just a park was, before its destruction by the Gestapo in 1943, the first Jewish cemetery in Berlin, originally established in 1672. Also the site of a Jewish old people's home, it was used as a detention centre by the Nazis, who held 55,000 Berlin Jews here before deportation. In 1990, a monument was erected, on which people place pebbles to show their respect. A little further on the tomb of the Jewish liberal philosopher Moses Mendelssohn can also be found.

5 Hackesche Höfe★★
Rosenthaler Straße, 40-41.

Built in the early 20th century and decorated with colourful ceramics in true Art Deco style, this succession of inner courtyards has taken over as the new centre of Berlin nightlife. In this microcosm resembling a miniature village, tourists and impassive regulars pass and observe one

another. As you move from courtyard to courtyard, from cafés to theatres, from modern galleries to designer showrooms, linger a while over the creations of the *Kostümhaus* designer and the art jeweller's *Schmuckwerk*.

6 Galerie Hoffmann★★
Sophienstraße, 21
☎ 28 49 91 21
Guided tours (charge made) Sat. by appointment.

Make your way under the new light installations into the *Sophie Gips Höfe*, where you come to the heart of an old factory that has been recently renovated and turned into studios, galleries and trendy cafés (give *Barcomi's* a try). Here, in their vast flat, the Hoffmanns display their

contemporary art collection, from the 'negatives' of Andy Warhol to the work of François Morellet.

7 Kunst-Werke★★
Auguststraße, 69
☎ 28 17 325
Tue.-Thu. and Sun. noon-6pm, Fri.-Sat. noon-9pm
Entry charge.

There are around twenty art galleries in this street, all of which stage events and exhibitions, making this a happening arts centre. From the outside there is nothing to suggest the existence of the *Bravo* café, masked by a glass sculpture by Dan Graham, in which, over a *Milchkaffee* and pastry, you can meditate on the avant-garde works and installations exhibited on the various floors of the gallery.

8 Al Contadino Sotto Le Stelle★★
Auguststraße, 34
☎ 28 19 023
Daily, 5pm-2am.

After strolling among the galleries and design studios of Auguststraße and Gipsstraße, there's nothing like breathing in a little Tuscan air. This young Italian restaurant opposite *Hackbarth's* attracts many locals. Its combination of rustic dishes and good wines are sure to make it known to a wider clientele pretty soon though.

9 Penthesileia★★
Tucholskystraße, 31
☎ 28 21 152
Mon.-Fri. 10am-7pm, Sat. 10am-4pm.

The leatherwork of these two young designers is inspired by Penthesileia, the queen of the Amazons of Greek mythology. Their brightly-coloured and beautifully crafted handbags and rucksacks (DM350) can take the forms of flowers, ladybirds and even porcupines. Ever generous, they allow one of their milliner friends to display his wonderful hats in the showroom.

10 Sophienstraße★
Running alongside the Sophienkirche, the street of the same name owes its architectural unity to the famous restorations undertaken by the GDR for the so-called 750th anniversary of the city. While they were careful

to restore the 18–19th-century houses in their original styles, special attention was paid to the 'craftsman's house' (no. 18, 1852). A former centre of militant Communism, it now houses galleries and workshops. Stop at no. 23 and have a drink at Whisky and Cigars.

⓫ Jubimal★
Tucholskystraße, 34
☎ 28 38 73 77
From 8pm.

The lack of sign and the blandness of the façade do nothing to betray the presence of a cocktail bar. This is a favourite haunt among the young trendies in the new fashionable district. The lively atmosphere is largely due to the rhythms dispensed by the various jazz quartets that perform here on Friday and Saturday evenings (from 10pm).

⓬ Ruby★
Oranienburger Straße, 32
☎ 28 38 60 30
Tue.-Fri. 11am-8pm,
Sat. 11am-6pm.

This furniture and accessory shop has taken up residence in the Heckmann

Höfe, a new series of inner courtyards bordering the new synagogue. The objects on display evoke minimalist Japanese interiors. If you want to treat yourself to something but would rather avoid anything too cumbersome, they have some lovely vases, dishes or incense burners.

⓭ Moove
Rosenthaler Straße, 28-31
☎ 28 38 65 61
Mon.-Sat. 10am-10pm.

If you like gadgets or inflatable armchairs and sofas, then this is the place for you.

If you really want to go home with a Berlin souvenir, ask where you can find the *Ampelmännchen*. These red and green figures were used on the pedestrian traffic lights of the former GDR and have been printed onto T-shirts or turned into Chinese lanterns (*see left*).

⓮ IN THE FOOTSTEPS OF BERTOLT BRECHT★★
From the Berliner Ensemble, where the première of the *The Threepenny Opera* was a smash hit in 1928, to no. 125 Chausseestraße, where he spent his last years (1953-1956), this is Brecht's district. His flat, which has been turned into a museum, overlooks the greenery of the Dorotheenstädtischer Friedhof, where he lies buried. Admirers can visit the bookshop where regular readings of his work are held.

Prenzlauer Berg, a place that's always buzzing

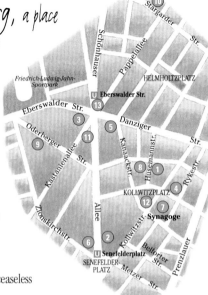

'I like to stroll through the streets of Berlin with no particular aim in mind, as real strolling requires.' This quip by the novelist Theodor Fontane takes on its full meaning in Prenzlauer Berg. Here you'll share the Berliners' nonchalance and meet the inhabitants of a *Kiez* (district) marked by its Jewish heritage, its working-class history and ceaseless artistic creation.

antique and secondhand shops. Expect to find furniture and objects from the 'foundation years' of the German empire (*Gründerzeit*). Rummage through the wares on offer at no. 7 and you may come up with a metal toy or old lamp that takes your fancy.

❷ Der Jüdische Friedhof★★

Schönhauser Allee, 23-25
Mon.-Thu. 8am-4pm,
Fri. 8am-4pm
Entry free.

❶ Husemann-straße★★

Husemannstraße was the museum street of Berlin in the late 19th century. It was restored at great cost by the East German regime to mark the 750th anniversary of the city in 1987 and is now home to a number of

an oasis of greenery where they can share a beer in the company of their family or friends. Prater Garten, the oldest *Biergarten* in Berlin stages artistic events attracting actors in rehearsal, students as well as local residents, often numbering over a thousand people in summer.

of ravioli) and concerts of Russian and Jewish music (every Tuesday at 8pm) are served in a peaceful setting. Opposite stands the water tower, the symbol of Prenzlauer Berg which is now inhabited. It dates from 1875 and has a sinister history since political prisoners were tortured here from 1933 onwards.

This cemetery is evidence of the presence in the district of a large Jewish community estimated at 20,000 people in 1925, a number reduced to 891 in 1945. It was opened in response to the law against burial in the city centre. Ask for a map at the entrance which will help you find your way through the maze of tombs, the most famous of which is that of the painter Max Liebermann.

🔞 Prater Garten★★
Kastanienallee, 7-9
☎ 448 56 88
In summer Mon.-Fri. from 4pm, Sat.-Sun. from noon, in winter Mon.-Fri. from 6pm, Sat.-Sun. from 2pm.

As soon as spring arrives, the Berliners seek out

❹ Pasternak★★
Knaackstraße, 24
☎ 441 33 99
Daily, 10-2am.

In the heart of the district peopled by the *Szene*, the *Pasternak* is popular both day and night. *Wareniki, pelmini, pierogi* (kinds

🔟 Kulturbrauerei★★
Knaackstraße, 97
☎ 441 92 69
Wed.-Sun. 2-9pm (exhibs.).

If you're looking for artists, this former brewery (1871-1889), which is currently being renovated, is where

they've sought refuge since 1990. Three galleries, a theatre, a concert hall and a disco bear witness to the vitality of the 'alternative' community. On Sundays, the attics house a flourishing clandestine flea market.

❻ Pfefferberg★★
Schönhauser Allee, 176
☎ 449 65 34.

It isn't that easy to deny one's industrial past, and a good thing, too! The former Pfeffer brewery, has been restyled as a place where music can flourish in the open air. The experimental exhibitions and events held on the terrace in May give

beer drinkers an alibi, and after dark, reggae, techno and jungle take over. It's the perfect place to get away from it all and dance the night away.

❼ Die Synagoge★
Rykestraße, 53
Closed to the public.

This synagogue has no particular architectural interest, but its presence in the heart of a district that suffered in the war serves as a reminder of a lost part of Berlin culture. Built between 1903-1904, it served as a school for Jewish children, but was obliged to close its doors in 1938. Although it escaped complete destruction following the violence of Kristallnacht, it was not restored until 1953.

❽ November★
Husemannstraße, 15
☎ 442 84 25
Daily, 10am-2pm.

This *Kneipe* with its navy blue decor at the top of Husemannstraße is a

very pleasant place to eat. The food just melts in your mouth (try the delicious courgette and salmon gratin) and the staff are friendly. It's warm and cosy in winter, when you can stay and read by the light of a candle. In summer, its quiet location makes it the ideal setting for a late breakfast. *Ein Milchkaffee, bitte!*

❾ Oderberger Straße★

Lying on the borders of Prenzlauer Berg, Mitte and Wedding, this street takes you back in time to the Berlin of the thirties. From October to March, the smell of coal can be strong but you can always take refuge in the *Kneipe Entweder Oder* (no. 15). You may prefer to take a look at the former public baths (no. 57-59), which are evidence of the architectural fashion at the turn of the century (1899-1902) for the canons of the German Renaissance. Then again, you may choose

---

⑫ KOLLWITZPLATZ AND KÄTHE KOLLWITZ★★

This square, surrounded by trees and houses with solid middle-class façades and the sculpture in its centre, both pay homage to the famous sculptress Käthe Kollwitz (1867-1945), who was a resident of the district. A friend of Rodin and Ernst Barlach, she displayed in her work an unfailing pacifism that was adopted by the GDR for its own ends. A remarkable museum is devoted to her in Charlottenburg (see p. 51).

KÄTHE-KOLLWITZ-MUSEUM
BERLIN
Fasanenstraße 24 · 10719 Berlin · Telefon 882 52 10

to stroll in the Mauerpark, ('Wall park') the last trace of the German division.

🔟 Headhunter★
Stargarderstraße, 76
Mon.-Fri. 11am-8pm,
Sat. 11am-4pm.

If you suddenly feel like a makeover, there's no need to make an appointment here. You can come whenever you like and listen to techno music while you wait your turn. You pay a fixed price (DM20) for whatever shampoo, cut or colour

you may choose. It's young and trendy and is situated opposite the *Gethsemane-kirche*, which was the centre of democratic protest. It's hard to believe that this peaceful street was once the site of police violence, when they ruthlessly beat anti-government demonstrators. During the course of 1989, people would come to the church to light a candle in support of the reforms that were beginning to be put in place.

🔟 Tonhalle
Kastanienallee, 96
☎ 440 47 599
Mon.-Fri. 11am-7pm,
Sat. 11am-4pm.

This tiny shop specialising in Berlin electronic music labels allows you to listen to drum 'n' bass, techno, jungle or big beat on their three record decks.

Even if you don't go away with the very latest mixes, the flyers you can pick up here will tell you where to head for an unforgettable night out. For fans of more traditional sounds, there's a shop called Da Capo at the same address which offers rock, jazz and a variety of international sounds, also on vinyl.

🔟 Konnopkes Imbiss
Schönhauser Allee, 44a
Mon.-Sat. 4.30-8pm.

Since the time of the GDR, this wooden hut, nestling under the iron arches of the U-Bahn, has been an institution for its delicious *Currywurst* (curried sausage). It's full from morning till night. Workers, locals and students come from far and wide to enjoy their favourite snack as well as other kinds of sausages. Ideal for a quick lunch.

Wilmersdorf, a suburban dream

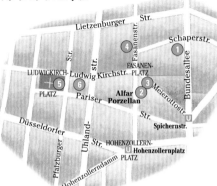

The natural extension of Charlottenburg with its shady streets and their elegant façades, Wilmersdorf perpetuates a certain art of living. The home of good taste and traditional art galleries, after nightfall the district becomes the haunt of young lawyers and financial advisers, bent on conspicuous consumption. In spite of this, it never fails to please. It's still the provincial Berlin of yesteryear and a pleasant place in which to wander.

Just a stone's throw from the School of Fine Art, you'll find one of the plushest

venues in Berlin, filled with a young, trendy clientele. Behind curtains which gleam in the candlelight reflected by hundreds of small mirrors, some of the best cabaret artists perfom in front of you. Dinner is a luxury you can perfectly well do without by reserving a 'Champagne Loge' where salmon canapés and champagne are naturally *de rigueur*.

❶ Bar Jeder Vernunft★★
Schaperstraße, 24
☎ 883 15 82
Tickets every day, noon-7pm.

❷ Alfar Porzellan★★
Fasanenstraße, 58
☎ 881 59 22
Mon.-Fri. 1-6.30pm,
Sat. 11am-2pm.

It may or may not be a deliberate homage to the ochre hues of the dark continent, but the vases, dishes (DM45) and other original designs by the two artists here borrow colours, patterns and a certain simplicity of style from Africa. Made and fired on the spot, the pieces wait patiently in line for visitors to admire and purchase them. There are some pieces of porcelain shaped like bamboo which are particularly impressive

❸ Mao Thaï★
Meierottostraße, 1
☎ 883 28 23

Mon.-Fri. noon-3pm,
5pm-midnight,
Sat.-Sun. 1pm-midnight.

For anyone who appreciates the delicate sweet and sour flavours of oriental cuisine, this Thai restaurant is the ideal place to come. Extremely popular with Berliners, this pretty restaurant serves beautifully presented dishes, the service is excellent and the staff are renowned for their polite attitude. A bit on the expensive side, it can get busy, so you are advised to book in advance.

❺ Ludwigkirchplatz★

You'd almost think you were in the centre of a village in this pretty little square. The fifty-year-old trees, attractive plants and the abundance of café terraces and a kind of provincial nonchalance all give the measure of a district where people take the time to enjoy life. To sample its charms, choose a table at Weyer's and watch the world go by, over a drink. Even the church of St Ludwig (1897) and its modest community of

Franciscan monks contribute in their own way to the relaxed lifestyle – the Sunday Mass takes place at midday, a rarity that attracts all the late rising night owls of the West.

❻ Manzini★
Ludwigkirchstraße, 11
☎ 885 31 41
Every day, 8-2am.

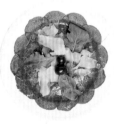

Half-way between a Viennese restaurant and an Italian café, this place is the plush rallying point for trendy forty-somethings and middle-class women with nothing much else to do. On fine days, you can have lunch or dinner here on the terrace, with dishes concocted by a different chef every week. The cuisine is more Mediterranean than German, but who's complaining?

GALERIE BREMER

❹ GALERIE BREMER & BAR★★
Fasanenstraße, 37 ☎ 881 49 08
Tue.-Fri. noon-6pm, Sat. 11am-1pm.
Bar Mon.-Sat. from 8pm.

A gallery by day and a bar by night could be a strange mixture, but this works very well. In 1955, Hans Scharoun personally designed the comfortable bar, with its red leather armchairs and low tables. In the semi-darkness, the paintings by modern artists create such a cosy atmosphere that you might almost find yourself holding forth on the subject of abstract art. But the cocktails that have flowed for over 45 years from the American shaker of Rudolf van der Lak are soon likely to put paid to any pretentions you may have.

Dahlem, life among lakes and museums

There could be no better illustration of a city in the country than Dahlem. Set among lakes and forests, this residential district made up of villas and museums is nevertheless very lively thanks to the university students who frequent it. As you enjoy the leafy peace and quiet, you're equally likely to come across young students, older people, or possibly even diplomats on their way to work.

❶ Museum für Völkerkunde★★★

Lansstraße, 8
☎ 20 90 55 55
Tue.-Fri. 10am-6pm,
Sat.-Sun. 11am-6pm
Entry charge.

This Museum of Ethnology comprises the following collections: Africa, American archeology, American ethnology, Europe, the Islamic Orient, eastern and northern Asia, South and South-east Asia, the South-Seas and Australia. With a total of 500,000 objects from around the world, this is one of the best museums of its kind. After extensive restoration work, the rooms of the various museums should be lighter and more majestic. The wealth of artefacts from non-European civilisations is vast and you're advised to pay special attention to the collection of Oceanic ships and the Mongolian yurts.

❷ Brücke Museum★★

Bussardsteig, 9
☎ 831 20 29
Wed.-Mon. 11am-5pm
Entry charge.

The standard bearer of the German Expressionist circle, the artistic community know

as 'Die Brücke' ('the bridge' owes this museum to the generosity of the painter Karl Schmidt-Rottluff, who donated his works to the city on his 80th birthday. Built in the Bauhaus style n the late 1960s, the building houses a unique collection of sculptures and paintings by artists such as Heckel or Kirchner, who were trying to create colourful worlds tinged with sentimentality.

❸ Jagdschloss Grunewald★★
Im Grunewaldsee, 29
☎ 813 35 97
May-Oct. Tue.-Sun.
10am-5pm, Nov.-Apr.
Sat.-Sun. 10am-4pm.
Entry charge.

This Baroque-style hunting lodge on the edge of Lake Grunewald contains the sole remaining example of the Berlin Renaissance, a state room decorated with a painted wooden ceiling, dated 1542. Though decorated with hunting trophies and fairly rustic, the lodge nevertheless contains a collection of around 200 paintings, including works by Cranach the Younger and Rubens. After this short cultural interlude, be sure to go for a walk round the lake and stop off at the terrace of the *Forsthaus Paulsborn* café.

❺ Chalet Suisse★
Im Jagen, 5
☎ 832 63 62
Every day,
11.30am-
midnight.

In the heart of the forest, mid-way between the lakes and the museums, this restaurant is an ideal place to stop on a hot summer's day. Tuck into one of the many *Spargel* (asparagus) dishes or a *Wiener Schnitzel* (Viennese escalope) and you'll soon feel refreshed and ready to face the ethnology museums.

❻ Alliierten-Museum★
Clayallee, 135
☎ 818 19 90
Every day, except Wed.
10am-6pm.
Entry free.

This museum on the site of the former American armed forces' cinema celebrates, perhaps a little too blatantly, the role of the Western Allies in the development of democracy in Germany. But it is certainly fascinating to see the American Air Force Dakota and the former Checkpoint Charlie border post. History buffs will be equally interested in the exhibition devoted to the Soviet blockade of the city which took place in 1948-1949.

❹ DOMÄNE DAHLEM★★
Königin-Luise-Straße, 49
☎ 832 50 00
Wed.-Mon. 10am-6pm
Entry charge, exc. on Wed.

This imposing farmhouse, which has been turned into an ecology museum and agricultural and craft centre, is all that remains of the former royal estate of Dahlem. If you aren't into organic produce, you can always go for a ride in a horse-drawn carriage in the surrounding area. This, and the village fetes that are regularly held here, make it a place children are sure to appreciate.

Rooms and restaurants
Practicalities

The fall of the Wall was accompanied by a boom in Berlin's hotels. In ten short years, new hotels have sprung up like mushrooms, mainly in anticipation of the government's move from Bonn to Berlin. Most of the recently-built or renovated hotels are unfortunately very expensive. A small, friendly pension or pension-hotel is a more affordable alternative.

RESERVATIONS

Despite the large number of hotels in Berlin, it's always advisable to make a reservation at least two months in advance when events such as fairs, festivals or the Love Parade are taking place. Outside these periods, and except for public holiday weekends, it's relatively easy to find a room just a week before departure.

The best way to make a reservation is to contact the hotel or pension direct. All you have to do is write, fax or phone the dates of your stay, the type of room you want and, in certain cases, your credit card number. In return, you'll receive a confirmation *(Bestätigung)* to sign and send back. You won't have to pay a deposit, but around 80% of the price of the room can be deducted from your account if you don't honour a reservation.

Since many hotels are now on the Internet, it's also possible to pay for your reservation by e-mail. The other possibility is to book through the Berlin tourist information office, which will reserve a room in the district of your choice for a commission. Unfortunately, their selection doesn't necessarily take the style, decor or originality of the hotels into account and often has a limited number of places available. However, they can provide you with a complete list of hotels on request.

Lastly, bear in mind that Berlin hotels haven't offered low season rates for two or three years. Some pensions and a few large hotels nevertheless offer weekend reductions. Don't forget to ask.

CLASSIFICATION

The classification of hotels by category is a very recent change in Berlin. However, it still isn't systematic and a large number of hotels that are either unaffiliated or awaiting classification haven't yet been awarded stars.

There are five categories, from the simple *Tourist*, to the more luxurious *First* and *Luxus*, by way of *Standard* and *Konfort* corresponding to international price, equipment and service standards. The price of the room generally includes a generous buffet breakfast.

CHOOSING A RESTAURANT

While Berlin isn't renowned for its gastronomic specialities, it nevertheless offers a considerable choice of very good multicultural restaurants, from Italian (most common) to Australian or Chinese. However, there are some restaurants and inns that serve excellent-quality traditional dishes.

The city also has many famous restaurants, which are often linked to well-known hotels (such as the *Palace* and *Residenz*), where you can enjoy a gourmet meal consisting of several courses. (*Gänge*). But in most restaurants the meal is limited to a main course, which is often very generous, accompanied by vegetables and sometimes a small side salad.

WHERE TO EAT

There are three main places to eat in Berlin – the *Imbiss*, a little stand where you can eat on the hop, the *Kneipe*, a sort of bistrot where you can eat, drink and chat, and the *Restaurant*, which is more prestigious and therefore more expensive. The *Kneipe* is an institution. It offers the best value for money and is definitely the most popular.

It has to be said that eating out in Berlin couldn't be more affordable. A good meal in a *Kneipe* won't cost you more than DM35 and the set meals of the large restaurants never cost more than DM200 per person.

MEALTIMES

Mealtimes aren't a problem in Berlin. Apart from a few restaurants, most places offer a choice of meals or snacks all day long. As the nightlife is particularly intense, some are happy to serve customers after midnight and many *Imbiss* stay open 24 hours a day.

TIPS

It isn't common practice to leave a tip on the table in Germany. When the waiter gives you the bill or tells you the price of your drink, it's up to you to round the amount up (usually by about 10%).

If you're paying by credit card, write the tip you want to leave on the bill and add up the total. Do check that the restaurant takes credit cards before ordering your meal, especially if you're in the old East Berlin.

HOTELS

Prenzlauer Berg

Haus Acksel

Belforterstraße, 21
☎ 44 33 76 33
🖷 441 61 16
DM99, not incl. breakfast.

This attractive, well-restored house is one of the few places offering accommodation in the vicinity of Kollwitzplatz. Each room is a self-contained apartment that is furnished simply but very tastefully, with cooking facilities and a small sitting-room. It's a real home from home for an incredibly reasonable price.

Hackescher Markt (Mitte)

Hotel Hackescher Markt★★★

Präsidentenstraße, 8
☎ 28 00 30
🖷 28 00 31 11
Email: Hohama@aol.com
Around DM250.

With its Classical façade, this comfortable hotel was the first of its kind to open in the trendiest part of Mitte. It's only a stone's throw from the Hackeschen Höfen and Oranienburgerstraße – in other words, at the heart of a district with some of the liveliest nightlife in the city.

EKOS Boardinghouse

Mulackstraße, 1
☎ 283 52 54
🖷 283 52 55
Around DM165, not incl. breakfast.

These brand-new flats in a quiet, charming street in Mitte are very pleasant indeed. They're light and spacious and you're sure to feel at home here, especially in the duplex on the top floor. In the evening, you can venture out into Mulackstraße and the surrounding area, where you'll find friendly, trendy cafés that remain undiscovered by tourists.

Schiffbauerdamm (Mitte)

Hotel Künstlerheim Luise

Luisenstraße, 19
☎ 280 69 41
🖷 280 69 42
Email: luise@compuserve.com
DM75-200.

The concept is a simple one. Artists were given *carte blanche* to design a room on a particular theme in this hotel, which is housed in a magnificent listed building. The result, which is sometimes surprising, is a great success and has transformed the hotel into a little gem within the means of all.

Hotel-Restaurant Albrechthof★★★

Albrechtstraße, 8
☎ 308 86 0
🖷 308 86 100
Around DM310.

Built between 1908 and 191[...] the Albrechthof is the oldest hot[...] in Berlin and certainly one of th[...] most charming in Mitte. I[...] location a stone's throw from th[...] Spree and the Berliner Ensem[...]ble makes it both very pleasa[...] and relatively central. The inn[...] courtyard, with its chapel, is th[...] perfect setting for a gourm[...] dinner for two on a summe[...] evening.

Friedrichstraße

The Westin Gran[...] Berlin★★★★★

Friedrichstraße, 158-164
☎ 20 27 0

20 27 33 62
round DM450.

ith its theatrical entrance, this
rge hotel in Friedrichstraße is
ry impressive. Upstairs, each
om has been designed in a
rticular style – Rococo (in
omage to Frederick the Great),
t Nouveau, Belle Époque or
on. Full of fin-de-siècle
mosphere, it's hard to believe
at this was once the most pres-
ious hotel in the GDR.

orint Select
otel am
endarmenmarkt ★★★★

arlottenstraße, 50-52
26 55 35 91
26 55 35 94
ound DM400.

Unter den Linden

Hotel Adlon
Kempinsky ★★★★★

Unter den Linden, 77
☎ 22 61-0
🕿 22 61 22 22
Around DM550, not incl.
breakfast.

In the first half of the 20th
century, the Adlon Hotel was
renowned throughout Europe
as the most luxurious hotel in
Berlin: its famous guests
included Einstein, Theodore
Roosevelt, Charlie Chaplin and
the young Marlene Dietrich.
Destroyed just after the war, the
widowed Frau Adlon raised the
necessary funds to build an
exact replica after the fall of the
Wall. The present hotel may not
have regained all the grandeur

e Dorint Select Hotel is a
vcomer to the splendid Gen-
menmarkt square. Meticu-
sly designed down to the last
il by a talented architect and
gner, it's sober, traditional
elegant. Ask for one of the
ms on the top floor. Their
all balconies with a view
he French and German
nedrals offer a uniquely
uresque setting.

of its predecessor, but parts such
as the lobby and grand staircase, will transport you back in
time. Its sense of history combined with its unique location
close to the Brandenburg Gate
have, in a short space of time,
made the Adlon once more the
choice of leading politicians and
international stars.

Potsdamer Platz

Madison

Potsdamerstraße, 3
☎ 590 05 00 00
🕿 590 05 05 00
Around DM230, not incl.
breakfast.

The Madison was one of the first
big hotels to open in the
redeveloped Potsdamer Platz.
Thanks to its central position,
it has an outstanding view of
the new complex, which is now
approaching completion. The
elegant rooms have all been
designed as spacious suites with
a desk and a kitchen area: the
Madison offers luxury at
remarkably low prices. The roof
terrace is a perfect spot for
breakfast or simply relaxing.

Märkisches Museum (Mitte)

Art'otel Ermelerhaus

Wallstraße, 70-73
☎ 240 62-0
🖷 240 62-222
Email:
reservation@artotel.de
Around DM300.

The Art'otel is a piece of very modern architecture that gives pride of place to the works of the German Neo-Expressionist artist Georg Baselitz. The Ermelerhaus adjacent to the hotel, on the other hand, is the oldest patrician house in Berlin, dating from 1567. Converted in the mid-18th century into a Rococo palace, this historical monument now houses a celebrated restaurant and has a majestic atrium which is ideal for breakfast. This very successful juxtaposition of modern art, architecture and design with an old palace will appeal both to lovers of tradition and fans of contemporary art alike.

Hotel Luisenhof

Köpenickerstraße, 92
☎ 241 59 06
🖷 279 29 83
Around DM280.

A stone's throw away from the Ermelerhaus, in the vicinity of the Nikolai district and Alexanderplatz, is the oldest block of flats in Berlin, built in 1822. Warm and welcoming, with small lounges and a fine spiral staircase, it was converted into a hotel in 1993 and still retains the feel of a private home. All the rooms have a traditional, understated elegance and the conservatory is the perfect place to get the day off to a gentle start.

Zoologischer Garten

Hotel Palace★★★★★

Im Europa Center
Budapesterstraße
☎ 25 02-0
🖷 25 02 11 61
Email: Hotel@palace.de
Around DM460.

Revamped throughout by London designer Erza Pavrir, this large hotel offers truly palatial accommodation. With individually decorated suites and marble bathrooms, everything seems to have been designed to be both relaxing and easy on the eye. To complete the picture, the hotel boasts one of the finest restaurants in Berlin, the First Floor, and a unique view of the zoo and Ku'damm as well.

Kurfürstendamm

Hotel Brandenburger Hof, Relais & Châteaux

Eislebenerstraße, 14
☎ 214 05-0
🖷 214 05-100
Email:
info@brandenburger-hof.com
Around DM380.

Situated in one of the quiet streets around the Ku'damm, the hotel is one of the few in the whole of Germany to belong to the exclusive Relais & Château group. With its majestic lobby columns, plasterwork and elegant, plant-filled conservatory, this superb turn-of-the-century building makes a wonderful setting for a stay in Berlin. A little gem of a restaurant, the Quadriga, is star-rated; it seats only 25 and you will need to book at least a week in advance.

Hotel Residenz

Meinekestraße, 9
☎ 884 43-0
🖷 882 47 26
Email:
info@hotel-residenz.com
Around DM250.

As soon as you cross the threshold of this marvellous Belle Époque building, you'll be plunged into an Art Nouveau atmosphere reminiscent of the 1900s. Decorative paintings, pastel colours and abundant stucco are the hallmarks of these very elegant, retro surroundings. The restaurant, Grand Cru, with its equally authentic atmosphere, will please aesthetes and gourmets alike.

Hotel Bleibtreu

Bleibtreustraße, 31
☎ 884 74-0
✆ 884 74-444
Email:
info@bleibtreu-hotel.com
Around DM310, breakfast
DM26.

To reach this charming hotel, you'll first have to make your way down an elegant little passage flanked by a florist's, a delicatessen and a bar, before crossing an unusual inner courtyard. Here you'll find the friendly and welcoming Bleibtreu, which is perfectly integrated with its surroundings. Colourful, original and refined, it's sure to delight all lovers of Italian design.

Pension Funk

Fasanenstraße, 69
☎ 882 71 93
✆ 883 33 29
Around DM110.

With its sumptuous entrance and authentic 1920s and 1930s furnishings, this pension –once the home of Asta Nielsen, a star of the silent screen –will take you back in time to interwar Berlin. Room 22, whose timeless charm will appeal to even the least nostalgically minded, is especially recommended.

Hotel-Pension Dittberner

Wielandstraße, 26
☎ 881 64 85
✆ 88 46 95-0
Around DM160
(credit cards
not accepted).

This pension has a wonderful collection of antiques, paintings and various objets d'art. The individually furnished rooms have an old-fashioned charm and the dining-room is an absolute gem. Ask for room 220 and you'll be able to enjoy your very own en-suite conservatory.

Kreuzberg

Riehmers Hofgarten

Yorckstraße, 83
☎ 780 98 800
✆ 780 98 808
Email: info@hotel-riehmers-
hofgarten.de
Around DM250.

Built in 1891 in a neo-Renaissance style, the Riehmers is one of the finest examples of Berlin bourgeois architecture.

During its recent refurbishment, its architect-designer sensitively and harmoniously integrated up-to-the-minute design and contemporary art into the setting of the old building. The rooms vary in size, but all are spacious; the decor combines pale wood and primary colours to pleasing effect.

Grunewald

The Ritz-Carlton Schloßhotel★★★★★

Brahmsstraße, 10
☎ 895 84-0
✆ 895 84-800
Around DM700.

This late 19th-century mansion in the chic residential district of Grunewald is without a doubt the most luxurious and prestigious hotel in Berlin. Its former guests have included Konrad Adenauer and Romy Schneider; today it is the chosen residence of international stars and royal couples. The sumptuous decor, which has been thought through down to the very last detail, is the work of international fashion designer Karl Lagerfeld.

Restaurants

Prenzlauer Berg

Pasternak

Knaackstraße, 22-24
☎ 441 33 99
Every day, 10-2am,
food served until midnight.

The atmosphere at the Pasternak will remind you of the importance of Berlin's Russian community in the 1920s. The cosy café-salon is a meeting-place for politicians and intellectuals, and is also a restaurant where, for a very modest price, you'll be served tasty Russian specialities. Try the favourite dish of the Russian writer Boris Pasternak, beef Stroganov.

Gugelhof

Knaackstraße, 37
☎ 442 92 29
Every day, 10-1am,
food served until midnight.

The Gugelhof is one of several chic, lively restaurants found around one of the most pleasant parts of Prenzlauer Berg, Kollwitzplatz. Besides a choice of German, Alsatian and French

dishes, the restaurant has an excellent and very affordable wine list.

Mao Thai

Wörtherstraße, 30
☎ 441 92 61
Every day, noon-11pm.

The reputation of this Thai restaurant has gone far beyond its local area. In a relaxed setting, you can sample subtly spiced dishes that are full of unusual flavours. But remember, booking is essential. Its equally famous subsidiary, the Kamala, is located in Mitte, at no. 28 Oranienburgerstraße.

Villa Groterjan

Milastraße, 2
☎ 440 67 55
Every day, 11am-midnight.

At the turn of the 20th century, this unusual neo-Romanesque building was one of Berlin's most well-renowned brasseries. Recently re-opened as a restaurant, it's still relatively unknown and is strongly recommended for its superb original setting and fish and game specialities that are typical of the region.

Hackescher Markt

Modellhut

Alte Schönhauserstraße, 28
☎ 283 55 11
Mon.-Sat. 6.30-11pm.

This chic Mitte restaurant in a former hat factory, is a successful combination of old GDR premises, up-to-the-minute design and 1930s bistrot atmosphere. As well as its unusual setting, the Modellhut is renowned for its refined, inventive seasonal cuisine, with dishes such as medallion of venison with blackcurrants, glazed shallots and broccoli.

Oranienburgerstr.

Oren

Oranienburgerstraße, 28
☎ 282 82 28
Every day, 10-1am.

Housed in an annexe of the big Mitte synagogue, this restaurant offers very good Jewish-Arabian and vegetarian cuisine, as well as a wide choice of fish. The beer comes from Israel and the wines from Golan. Because of its location in a Jewish cultural centre and its highly individual atmosphere, it attracts a varied, cosmopolitan clientele.

Kellerrestaurant Brechthaus

Chausseestraße, 125
☎ 282 38 43
Every day from 6pm,
in summer noon-1am,
food served noon-3pm,
6-9pm.

In the cellar of Bertolt Brecht's former house, the Kellerrestaurant is now a gastronomical homage to the great writer. The Austrian-inspired dishes are said to be based on recipes originally cooked by Helene Weigel, Brecht's wife. The interior is full of period photos and is decorated with models of stage sets made by the master himself for the Berliner Ensemble – an absolute must-see. In

summer the inner courtyard is a truly delightful setting adjacent to the famous Dorotheenstädtischer cemetery (see p. 26).

Blue Goût

Anklamerstraße, 38
☎ 448 58 40
Mon.-Fri. noon-3pm,
7-11.30pm,
Sat.-Sun. 7-11.30pm.

Located in the rear courtyard of a former cosmetics factory, this restaurant has rapidly gained a reputation that reaches well beyond its immediate vicinity. You'll be pleasantly surprised by the originality and flavours of the Italian, Austrian and occasionally French-inspired cuisine. Blue Goût's imminent move to no. 8, Chausseestraße should further seal its success.

Schiffbauerdamm

Ständige Vertretung (StäV)

Schiffbauerdamm, 8
☎ 285 98 735
Every day, 11am-midnight.

Its walls are lined with photos dating from the time of the Bonn government, as this restaurant was originally aimed at Bonn government officials visiting Berlin. Having become increasingly popular, it has reached the happy compromise of offering dishes from both Berlin and the Rhineland. Try the delicious Berlin-style flambéed tart (*Flammenkuchen*).

Gendarmenmarkt

Borchardt

Französischestraße, 47
☎ 20 38 71 17
Every day, 11.30-1am.

With its imposing marble columns and period mosaics, the Borchardt has a strong turn-of-the-century atmosphere. This restaurant, which is reminiscent of La Coupole in Paris, was the first in Berlin to be designed on a Parisian model. Popular with politicians, the Borchardt is known for its fine, French-influenced cuisine.

Vau

Jägerstraße, 53-54
☎ 20 29 730
Mon.-Sat. noon-3pm,
7pm-1am.

The Vau is one of the most
fashionable new restaurants
in Berlin, serving subtle dishes
in a sober, elegant
setting. It owes its
reputation to chef
Anton Viehauser,
who has achieved a
refined, inventive
blend of traditional
Brandenburg recipes
and nouvelle cuisine.
It's worth knowing that
everything costs DM20 at
lunchtime.

Friedrichstraße Station

Zwölf Apostel

Georgenstraße, 177-180
☎ 201 02 22
Every day, 9-1am.

You'll be pleasantly
surprised by this Italian
trattoria, with its giant
murals and big chandeliers.
The pizzas here are thin and
crispy and quite delicious.
From midday to 6pm, they're
all half price. There's another
Zwölf Apostel restaurant, with
an equally Italianate decor,
in Charlottenburg, at no. 49
Bleibtreustraße.

Unter den Linden

Möwe

Am Festungsgraben, 1
☎ 201 20 29
Mon.-Sat. 6-11pm.

This restaurant owes its name
to the GDR's most famous
circle of
artists,
who used
to meet
in these
rooms on
the first
floor of
an elegant
palace. In
order to carry
on the tradition,
every Monday the
Möwe stages perform-
ances by musicians,
lyric artists and cabaret
singers to accompany
you while you eat
your meal
(DM60, in-
c l u d i n g
drink). All
very enjoyable.
In summer, the overhanging
terrace is a delightful spot.

Nikolaiviertel

Mutter Hoppe

Rathausstraße, 21
☎ 241 56 25
Every day, from 11.30am.

For anyone who wants to
sample genuine German cuisine while soaking up the atmosphere of Berlin, the Mutter
Hoppe is the perfect place to
come. It is very popular with
Berliners, and you'll find high-
quality dishes cooked the
traditional way. The goulash
with wild mushrooms and
cream is particularly delicious.

Reinhard's

Poststraße, 28
☎ 242 52 95
Every day, 9-1am.

Less traditional, more 1980s,
Reinhard's is renowned for its
moderately priced, high-quality
food. The *Geheimnis aus dem
Kaiserhof*, a tender steak accompanied by a delicate sauce
specially created for the Berlin
painter Max Liebermann, is
highly recommended (DM33).

Kreuzberg

Altes Zollhaus

Carl-Herz-Ufer, 30
☎ 692 33 00
Tue.-Sat. 6-11pm.

This former customs post in
an enchanting location by the
banks of the Landwehrkanal
is undoubtedly one of the
best restaurants in the city.
Its chef, Hebert Betle, serves
local cuisine that's light
and tasty. The smoked salmon
(*räucher lachs*) on a bed of

warm potatoes and the Brandenburg duck (*Ente*) shouldn't be missed. Set menus start at around DM65.

Abendmahl
Muskauerstraße, 9
☎ 612 51 70
Every day, 6pm-1am.

The name *Abendmahl*, meaning 'The Last Supper', is a reference to Leonardo da Vinci's famous painting. Often frequented by a gay clientele, this restaurant is – perhaps surprisingly – not at all kitsch. It offers absolutely exquisite fish and vegetarian dishes.

Austria
Bergmannstraße, 30
☎ 694 44 40
Every day, 6pm-1am.

This is one of the best Austrian restaurants in Berlin, serving tasty, authentic Austrian dishes. In addition to its excellent food and friendly welcome, the restaurant is worth visiting for its great location in one of the most charming squares in Berlin.

Savignyplatz

Filou
Bleibtreustraße, 7
☎ 313 55 43
Every day, 7pm-1am.

Situated in one of the most pleasant streets in the neighbourhood of the Ku'damm, the Filou is a real find. Its warm, intimate setting, the Morena and Ravenna tableware and, of course, the wonderful cooking aromas, with very tasty dishes cooked to traditional family recipes, are sure to please.

Paris Bar
Kantstraße, 152
☎ 313 80 52
Every day, noon-2am.

It's hard to decide whether it's the simple, high-quality French cuisine or the countless paintings on the walls that

are the main attraction here. One thing's for sure – in a few decades this unpretentious bistrot has become one of the most famous restaurants in Berlin – and its prices have risen accordingly. The haunt of leading politicians, writers and Hollywood stars during the film festival, it's become something of a legend. If you want to eat here, you'd be well advised to book in advance.

Kurfürstendamm

Bovril
Kurfürstendamm, 184
☎ 881 84 61
Mon.-Sat. 10-2am.

This simple, stylish café-bistrot is a Berlin institution that has for some years attracted an extremely varied clientele of artists, intellectuals, regulars, businessmen, film stars and tourists. Its cuisine is every bit as varied, ranging from the traditional breaded veal escalope to the most intricate of dishes. In summer the much sought-after terrace is one of the most elegant on the Ku'damm.

Mirnink
Kempinski Plaza
Ahlandstraße, 181/183
☎ 882 48 62
Bistrot from 9am, sushi and restaurant from noon.

This fish restaurant behind the Kempinski Hotel has recently had a makeover. Formerly known as the Fischküche, it's now called the Mirnink and is an unusual but highly successful combination of fish restaurant, sushi bar and Russian patisserie – an original and cosmopolitan mixture that reflects the many cultures that live side by side in this city.

IMBISSE

Freßco

Oranienburgerstraße, 48-49
☎ 282 96 47
Every day, 10-1am.

This Mitte café-*Imbiss* serves delicious vegetable tarts (DM5 a portion). You'll also find all sorts of Italian and Spanish snacks here, but bear in mind there is standing room only. Its location opposite the Tacheles makes it an ideal place to soak up the life of the district.

Bagel's and Daly

Rosenthalerstraße, 46-48
Every day, 8-3am.

In this very pleasant Mitte *Imbiss* you'll find a good choice of sandwiches, delicious Lebanese *schawarma* (lamb in pitta bread) and, of course, bagels, the chewy, ring-shaped Jewish rolls. You can ask for them lightly toasted and spread with taramasalata, cream cheese or avocado, or garnished with tomatoes, basil and mozzarella.

Hasir

Adalberstraße, 10
☎ 614 23 73
Open 24 hours.

With its Turkish population, Kreuzberg is *the* place to come for *doner kebab* – you'll find the best in the city here. Among the countless *Imbisse* serving kebabs, the Hasir is one of the most famous in the district for its generous portions, tasty Turkish *doner* and lentil soup (*Linsensuppe*).

Habibi

Goltzstraße, 24
Open from 11am until late at night.

The Habibi is unquestionably the most popular Lebanese *Imbiss* in Berlin. There's always a queue outside it, even late at night. The house speciality is a dish of *falafels* (DM5) accompanied by pitta bread and mixed salad.

Soup-Kultur

Kurfürstendamm, 224
☎ 88 62 92 82
Sun.-Fri. 11am-8pm,
Sat.11am-4pm.

This fashionable little place with its pop decor is part of the brand-new generation of Berlin *Imbisse*. You won't find kebabs or *Currywurst* here; instead there are delicious soups made to traditional recipes from around the world. To eat in or take away, they're all highly recommended. In summer, there are cold soups as well hot ones.

CAFÉS AND TEAROOMS

Barcomi's

Sophienstraße, 21 (Mitte)
☎ 694 81 38
Mon.-Sat. 9am-midnight,
Sun. and holidays. 10am-midnight.

For gourmets and foodies who'd like to sample coffee from the four corners of the earth or tuck into delicious bagels, muffins, brownies and home-made cookies (DM5), this café is highly recommended. There's another branch of Barcomi's in the Kreuzberg district, at no. 21 Bergmannstraße.

Tadschikische Teestube

Palais am Festungsgraben, 1 (Mitte)
☎ 204 11 12
Mon.-Fri. 5pm-midnight, Sat.-Sun. 3pm-midnight.

Tucked away on the first floor of an old palace, this unusual tea room with its authentic Tadjikistan decor invites you to celebrate the Russian tea ceremony according to the book. This means removing your shoes and sitting on the comfortable carpets. To accompany your tea you can order a Russian speciality or a more everyday snack.

Café Einstein

Kurfürstenstraße, 58 (Tiergarten)
☎ 261 50 96
Every day, 10-2am.

This Viennese-style café-restaurant has become a Berlin institution. The elegant turn-of-the-century villa, with its terrace and small garden, is most certainly an idyllic spot in which to have breakfast, sample the café's famous apple strudel or enjoy a delicious dinner.

Pasticceria Italiana

Leibnizstraße, 45 (Charlottenburg)
☎ 324 83 89
Every day, noon-10pm.

In this elegant tea room, every cake is a work of art. They are served plain or coated in a delicious fruit coulis, just as you prefer. A real treat.

Café im Literaturhaus

Fasanenstraße, 23
☎ 88 35 414
Every day, 9.30am-midnight.

With its shaded courtyard and wonderful conservatory area, this literary café in a beautiful 19th-century villa is a haven of peace, not far from the big avenues. Artists and intellectuals come here to listen to readings or simply drink coffee. You can have a meal here, too.

Café Übersee

Paul-Linke-Ufer, 44 (Kreuzberg)
☎ 618 87 65
Every day, from 10am.

On this idyllic bank of the Landwehrkanal you'll find a whole series of charming café-restaurants. The Café Übersee is perhaps the favourite among them. People come here to drink coffee, read the newspaper or, even as late as 4pm, to have one of those amazing German breakfasts.

Savarin

Kulmerstraße, 1
☎ 216 38 64
Every day, 10am-midnight.

The Savarin is known throughout Berlin for its outstanding cakes. There's also a wide choice of teas to accompany them.

A **B**

← Spree

OlbersStr.

L. Meitnerstr.

Gaußstr.

Charlottenburge

Tegeler

Osnabrücker Str.

MIERENDORFF

Kaiserin

Ⓤ Mierendorff Pl.

A 100

Weg

Mierendorffstr.

Sommeringstr.

①

Sophie-

Schlossgarten

← Spree

Winterstein Str.

Alt
Lietzow

Lütge

**Schloss
Charlottenburg**

LUISEN
PL.

Otto

Alt
LIETZOW

Gue

Spandauer

Damm

KLAUSENER
PL.

**Ägyptisches
Museum**

Winterstorfer Str.

R. WAGNER
PL.

Rathaus

Suhr

Ⓢ Westend

GIERKEPL.

R. Wagner

Wagner

Ⓤ R. Wagner

Christ-

str.

Schloss-

Kaiser-

Friedrich-

Zille-

Str.

**Deutsche
Oper**

Seelingstr.

Charlotten-

Danckelmannstr.

CHARLOTTENBURG

str.

str.

Friersche

②

Knobelsdorff-

str.

str.

SOPHIE
CHARLOTTE
PL.

Bismarck-

Ⓤ Bismarck
Str.

Ⓤ **Deutsche
Oper**

str.

Ⓤ Kaiserdamm

**Sophie Charlotte
Pl.**

Krumme

str.

Kaiserdamm

WITZLEBEN
PL.

Schiller-

St Thoma

Lietzenseepark

Wundt-

Lietzensee

Witzleben-

str.

Straße

KARL
AUGUST
PL.

Goe

Ⓢ **Witzleben**

Windscheidstr.

Pestalozzi-

Trinitatis K

Neue

Dernburg-

Kant-

AMTSGERICHT-
PL.

str.

Ⓤ **Wilmersdorfer
Str.**

Herbart-

Suarez-

Leonhardt-
str.

STUTTGARTER
PL.

Niebuhr-

str.

Ⓟ Ⓢ

Leibniz-

str.

Rönnerstr.

Charlottenburg

Mommsen-

Ⓢ **Westkreuz**

Gervinusstr.

HOLTZENDORFF
PL.

Sybel-

str.

MEYERINCK
PL.

Hellbronner

G. Wilhelm-
str.

Karlsruher

Damaschke Str.

Dahlmann Str.

Lewishamstr.

Ⓤ Adenauerpl.
ADENAUER
PL.

Kurfü

③

str.

Str.

Nestor-

str.

Xantenerstr.

Brandenburgische

Pa

Kurfürsten-

Friedrich

Cicero-

damm

Str.

Du sseld

Halensee

RATHENAU
PL.

Ⓢ **Halensee**

Westfälische

HOCHMEISTER
PL.

Eisenzahn-

Konstanzer

WILMERSDOR

Koenigsallee

Seesener Str.

Paulsborner

Str.

Konstanzer

Ⓤ Konstanzer P

A 100

A **B**

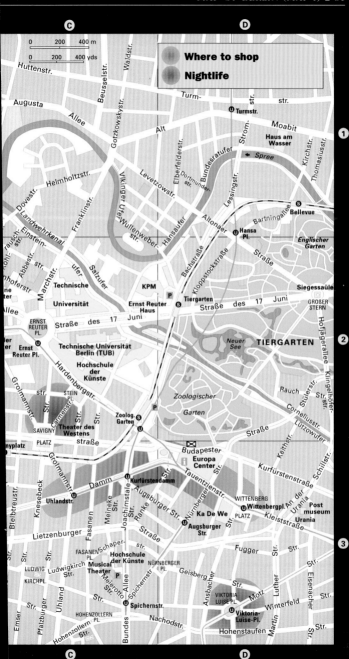

Where to shop

Nightlife

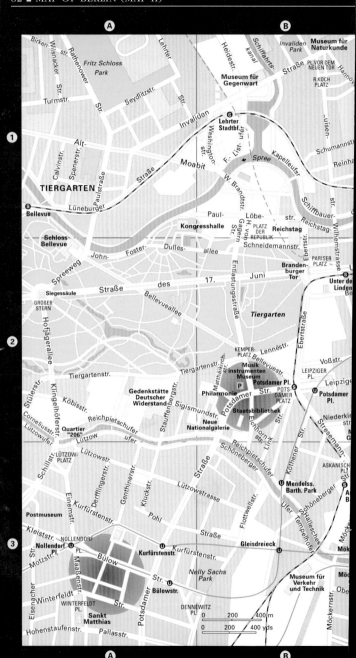

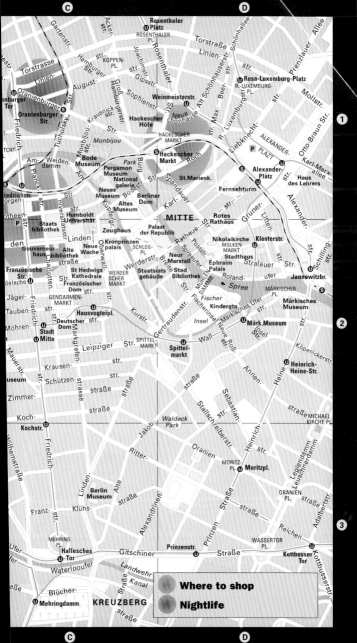

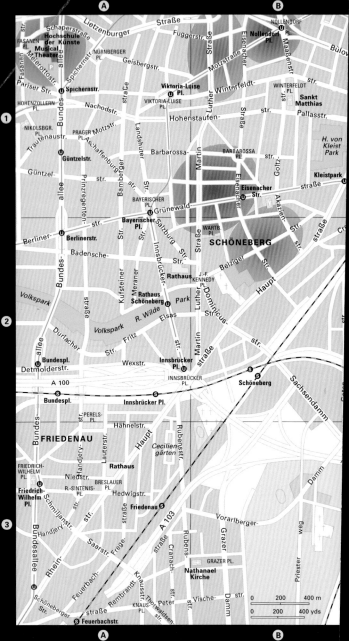

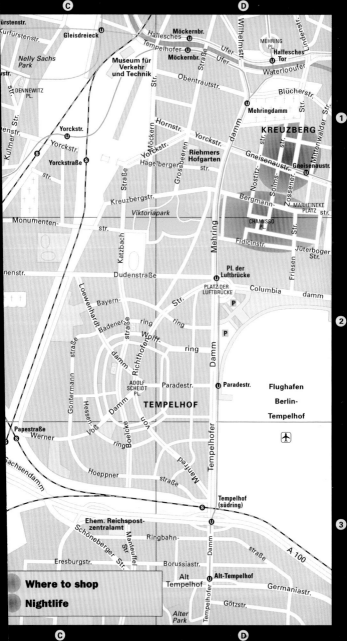

shopping Practicalities

Every district in Berlin specialises in a different type of shopping. Take advantage of this diversity to move from luxury shops to obscure alternative market stalls. Designers of every kind have always drawn their inspiration from this clash of opposites and so can you.

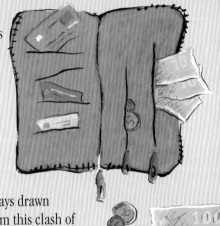

OPENING TIMES

Most shops are open Monday to Friday 10am to 8pm (an hour earlier in the morning for food shops and larger stores), and on Saturdays from 11am to 4pm, and sometimes 6pm in shopping arcades. Only the flea markets are open on Sundays.

WHERE TO SHOP

In Charlottenburg, the well-known designers, jewellers and other luxury shops are to be found in the Kurfürstendamm ('Ku'damm') and adjacent streets. Tauentzienstraße, which is the continuation of the Ku'damm, has a large number of department stores and international shops. Also in the west, in Schöneberg, around the Winterfeldplatz, many interior design and small trendy shops have congregated. In Kreuzberg, on Bergmannstraße, you'll find a wide choice of secondhand and junk shops. In the east, in Mitte, the latest fashionable district, you can choose from the luxurious boutiques around Friedrichstraße, and the young stylists and designers in the Spandauer Vorstadt and Scheunenviertel.

PAYING FOR YOUR PURCHASES

Cash is still the usual means of paying for purchases, though international credit cards are becoming more and more widely accepted by shopkeepers. Most of the time, a credit card is necessary to get cash and safer than carrying large sums of money around with you).

If your card is lost or stolen, call ☎ 069 74 09 87 for Eurocheque cards (EC) ☎ 069 263 88 88 for all other credit cards.

Traveller's cheques drawn in deutschmarks are rarely accepted in shops, but they'll allow you to withdraw money from banks. The Germans have a preference for Eurocheques (EC), for which a payment card, called an *EC-Karte*, is needed. Anyone who has a bank account in a European bank can ask for one in his or her country of origin.

BARGAINING

Prices are displayed everywhere in Berlin and bargaining isn't the done thing – except in the flea markets where, according to the stallholder's mood and your own talent, you may be able to negotiate a 20 or 30 per cent reduction. If you're hoping to get a bargain, it's a good idea to make a note of anything you like in the morning and then go back again at the end of the day before closing time. That way, you'll have the best chance of getting a good deal, if your bargain hasn't been snapped up by someone else, of course!

SALES

Sales occur twice yearly. The first, called the *Winterschlußverkauf* (WSV), starts on the last Monday in January and lasts 10 days. The second, called the *Sommerschlußverkauf* (SSV), starts on the last Monday in July and also lasts 10 days. Only clothes are involved, but prices may be reduced by as much as 75%. However, you'll find special offers are available throughout the year on computer, hi-fi and video equipment.

CUSTOMS

Duty-free sales between EU countries were abolished in 1999 and are now only available between Belgium and non-EU countries. If you're a citizen of a member state of the European Union, you won't have to pay any customs duty when you cross the frontier, though you may be asked to produce a list of the goods you're transporting, together with receipts showing that you paid duty on your purchases in Germany. This is all that's required, whatever the value of the goods you're bringing back. If you aren't an EU citizen, and if the value of your purchase exceeds DM 1,600, there are customs formalities to complete. If you've bought a work of art of cultural value (*Kulturgüter*), you have to obtain an exit permit (Brunnenstraße, 188-190 ☎ 285 25 0). However, you still need the receipt for your purchase. You may be asked to produce it by Customs and it will be useful should you ever wish to sell your purchase or are burgled and need to complete an insurance claim form.

FINDING YOUR WAY

Next to each address in the Shopping and Nightlife sections we have given its location on the maps of Berlin on pages 80-85.

Customs
Grellstraße, 16-31
☎ 42 43-5

Mehringdamm, 129c
☎ 690 09-01.

TRANSPORT

If you buy an item of furniture, a valuable work of art or simply a bulky object, you can have it delivered without any difficulty. You can send it either by air, which is quick but expensive, or, if you're delivering it within Europe, by road. Insurance cover is almost always included in the transportation charge.

Hertling
☎ 320 90 320.

UPS, United Parcel Service freephone number
☎ 0800 82 66 30.

Pietsch
☎ 84 57 120.

WOMEN'S FASHION

Like Berlin itself, German fashion draws on a multitude of stylistic references as it seeks to define itself. If you know where to look you'll find many workshops and young designers seeking recognition. Take advantage of this fever of creativity and check out the new talent. Bear in mind that there is no single predominant style and that eclecticism is the order of the day.

Anette Peterman
**Bleibtreustraße, 49
(map I, C3)
☎ 323 25 56
Mon.-Wed. 11am-7pm,
Thu.-Fri. noon-8pm,
Sat. 10am-4pm
U-Bahn Savignyplatz.**

This self-taught figure of the Berlin fashion world fearlessly tackles a different theme for each new collection. Taking her inspiration from the sirens of the silver screen, she designed diaphanous outfits (DM700-900) stitched with greyish-blue pearls. Her creations are divided into two lines: 'Classics' and 'Parallel'. The first, with its masculine influence, has an androgynous style. The second is more extravagant, sometimes mixing wool and silk in the same garment.

Veronica Pohle
**Schlüterstraße, 46
(map I, C2-3)
☎ 883 37 31
Mon.-Fri. 10am-8pm,
Sat. 11am-4pm
U-Bahn Adenauer Platz.**

Forget for a moment the conventional coldness of most contemporary designers establishments and enter the comforting warmth of Veronica Pohle's shop. The stucco ceilings and pink-papered walls make a glowing backdrop for the extravagant fashions of Christian Lacroix and Jean-Paul Gaultier. There are also accessories, bags, hats and jewellery byKenzo

Essenbeck
**Auguststraße, 72 (map II, C1)
☎ 28 38 87 25
Mon.-Fri. noon-8pm,
Sat. 11am-4pm
U-Bahn Oranienburger Straße.**

If you like contemporary cuts and fabrics, you'll find the clothes here are out of this world. The colour palette is chiefly restricted to black, white and grey. The well-heeled clientele particularly appreciates the wide range of streetwear by Austrian designer Helmut Lang. Between the printed T-shirts (DM75) and the white cotton avant-garde outfits (DM840), this shop is sure to have the very item you need to transform your wardrobe.

and Moschino.
the light of the
crystal chandeliers
is very flattering.

Ultramarin

Wörtherstraße, 33
(off map)
☎ 441 87 94
Mon.-Fri. noon-9pm,
Sat. 11am-4pm
U-Bahn Senefelderplatz.

If you have fairly eclectic
tastes and refuse to be
pigeon-holed into following
any particular style, then
this is the place for you.
Both a showroom and a
shop, Ultramarin houses
the latest collections
of a number of Berlin
designers, with silky
evening dresses displayed
alongside more casual
linen outfits.

Groopie Deluxe

Goltzstraße, 39
(map III, B1)
☎ 217 20 38
Mon.-Fri. 11am-8pm,
Sat. 11am-4pm
U-Bahn Nollendorfplatz.

This shop, in one of Schöneberg's
main shopping streets, is the

place to come for those
who wouldn't dream of
venturing into the clubs
without all the latest gear.
Fashionable clubwear
from the fertile
imaginations of
rising young
designers
puts the
accent on
citrus colours
and shiny accessories.
Whatever you choose
you'll create a
sensation.

Jil Sander

Kurfürstendamm,
185
(map I, B3)
☎ 886 70 20
Mon.-Fri. 10am-7pm,
Sat. 10am-4pm
U-Bahn Adenauer
Platz.

Sobriety is the
watchword of the
first lady
of German
ready-to-
wear
fashion.
In her stylish
shop on the Ku'damm
you'll find little or no bright
colours, only subtle shades of
cream, grey, black and camel.
The same spirit of sobriety
governs the cut, which is severe
and minimalist but effective.
To complete your outfit, there's
also a leather goods and shoe
department.

Stephanie Schenck

Gipsstraße, 9 (map II, C1)
☎ 28 39 07 85
Mon.-Fri. noon-8pm,
Sat. noon-4pm
U-Bahn Weinmeisterstraße.

In a former butcher's shop
converted into a workshop,
Stephanie Schenck gives pride
of place to colourful knitwear.
With the accent on silk and linen
mixtures, she creates low-necked
jumpers in a variety of pastel
shades (DM280). Her sheath
dresses are made in the darker
tones that accentuate soft
feminine curves.

CLOTHES & SHOE SIZES

Don't forget that on the
continent clothes and shoe
sizes are different from what
you may be used to, but the
sales assistant should be able
to help you find the perfect fit.
To help you navigate your way
through the different choices we
have included conversion tables
on page 128. These list not only
clothes and shoe sizes, but also
weights and measurements.

Molotow

**Gneisenaustraße, 112
(map III, D1)
☎ 693 08 18
Mon.-Fri. 2-8pm,
Sat. 10am-4pm
U-Bahn
Mehringdamm.**

Arno Karge's efforts
on behalf of Berlin
fashion have
never flagged.
Having organised
the shows of
the 'alternative'
scene in the 1980s,
his shop space
has always been
devoted to Berlin
designers, both
established and
up-and-coming.
The labels
Blackwithe, Quasi
Moda, Oware and P.O.S.H. are
only the tip of the iceberg,
which includes over 80 exciting
designers. This means there's
always plenty on offer to suit
all tastes.

Max & Co.

**Quartier 207 (map II, C2)
Friedrichstraße, 78
☎ 20 94 73 90
Mon.-Fri. 10am-8pm,
Sat. 10am-4pm
U-Bahn Französische Straße.**

Max Mara's attractive young
subsidiary displays perfect
examples of international fashion,
with lots of black effectively set
off by accessories in various
shades of purple, almond green
and crimson. the dresses
(DM190) are cut very close to the
body to show their wearers off
to advantage. Women executives
from the new business district
form the shop's loyal regular
clientele, knowing that they
will always be able to find the
perfect silk jacket or bolero
(DM150) to underline their
success in a man's world. Join
them and you, too, could find
what you're looking for.

Guru

**Münzstraße, 23
(map II, D1)
☎ 281 90 01
Mon.-Fri. noon-7pm,
Sat. 11am-4pm
U-Bahn Weinmeisterstraße.**

The home of Multikulti (a
mixture of cultures), Berlin is
alive with the sound of Afro-
American music. if you're
planning to go dancing to the
frenzied rhythms of salsa or any of
the other sounds of world music,
come to Guru first. fun fabrics,
tropical fashions and amulets will
give you the ideal excuse to turn
yourself into a hippie.

Antonie Setzer

**Bleibtreustraße, 19
(map I, C3)
☎ 883 13 50
Mon.-Wed. 10am-
7pm, Thu.-Fri. 10am-
8pm, Sat. 10am-4pm
U-Bahn Uhlandstraße.**

Black strikes again! But in a
plain, minimalist setting, this
designer understands the need
for contrasts. Simple and refined
to the extreme, the dresses
(DM600-700), blouses and
trousers reveal their full beauty
when matched with the deep
red scarves and jumpers. If you
go for the *femme fatale* look,
you'll feel at home here.

WOMEN'S FASHION ■ 91

Ute Lindner

Auguststraße, 52
(map II, C1)
☎ 30 87 20 45
Mon.-Fri. 11am-7.30pm,
Sat. 11am-3pm
U-Bahn Weinmeisterstraße.

With only clothes rails for
furniture, Ute Lindner's
simple showroom has a
feeling of neutrality and
spaciousness. With
her minimalist
approach,
and beautifully-cut separates,
the designer is responding to
clients who prefer the under-stated
to the obvious, without neglecting
quality and originality. The
clothes are generously cut and
the colours are never too
bright, even in summer.
A discreetly elegant trouser
suit sells for DM800 and a
classic white blouse for
DM180.

skin. Dresses, usually
designed in cotton or
wool, often sport
mandarin collars and
may be decorated with
little wooden clasps.
A slightly severe line
for women with a taste
for simple, elegant
lines.

Claudia Skoda

Kurfürstendamm, 50
(map I, C3)
☎ 885 10 09
Mon.-Fri. 11am-7pm,
Sat. 11am-4pm
U-Bahn Uhlandstraße.

There is perhaps a hint of
Japanese influence
in the collection by
Claudia Skoda. Her fine
knitwear fits like a second

Hut Up

Heckmann Höfe (map II, C1)
Oranienburger Straße, 32
☎ 28 38 61 05
Mon.-Fri. 11am-6pm,
Sat. noon-4pm
U-Bahn Oranienburger Straße.

Young designer Christine Birkle
has made a sensational start in
Berlin fashion. Preferring to
work in wool, she reveals its
unsuspected richness and variety.
Between the fine alpaca dress
(DM380) and the Irish or
Mongolian curled wool hat
(DM340), you can never quite
believe it's the same material.
However, her garments all convey
the same spring-like feel, a
freshness and lightness that
make them a pleasure to wear.

TAGEBAU

Rosenthaler Straße, 19
(map II, C-D1)
☎ 283 90 890
Mon.-Sat. 11am-8pm
U-Bahn Weinmeisterstraße

The workshops of the
six designers are linked
to the gallery, where you'll
make your way between
straw hats (DM300), jewellery
straight from the steppes of
Central Asia and translucent
plastic furniture. Your

attention may be grabbed by
the polythene dresses (DM350) or the 1950s-style suits, with their
nipped-in waists. Fashion is definitely experimental here. Whether
the garments can ever be worn is a secondary consideration.

FASHION ACCESSORIES

More than any other German city, Berlin is teeming with young designers. They're occasionally eccentric but always inventive. They don't set out to dress Mrs Average and make it a point of honour to hijack the latest fashion trends and break new ground. Hats, jewellery, underwear – they'll grab any excuse to let their imaginations run riot. If you'd rather play safe, you can always stick to the more traditional designers in the west of the city.

Orlando

**Oranienburger Straße, 7
(map II, C-D1)
☎ 281 98 38
Mon.-Fri. 11am-8pm,
Sat. 11am-4pm
U-Bahn Hackescher Markt.**

The interior decor of this shoeshop is something to be seen – a flame-covered wall with an iron ramp across it leads to the back of the shop. Here you'll find shoes in all the latest styles, from black leather to beige fabric platform shoes in sporty shapes (from DM129). When you find a pair that you just can't resist, you can perch on a chair from a 1950s hairdressing salon while you try them on.

Fishbelly

**Grunewaldstraße, 71a
(map III, B1)
☎ 788 30 15
Tue.-Fri. 1-7pm,
Sat. noon-4pm
U-Bahn Eisenacher
Straße.**

Say goodbye to boring underwear! Young designer Jutta Teschner's lingerie is a marvellous illustration of her slogan: 'Sexy clothes for sexy women'. Some of the underwear is seriously wicked, but alongside the extravagant sets designed for the bedroom (DM300-500), there are slightly more understated nighties and bras (from DM80) that will bring a touch of chic eroticism to your everyday life.

Tizian

**Kurfürstendamm, 187
(map I, C3)
☎ 88 50 01 80
Mon.-Fri. 10am-8pm,
Sat. 10am-4pm
U-Bahn Uhlandstraße.**

Bringing together all the classic shoe designers in one shop is one way to guarantee success. Especially when the address is known to all self-respecting West Berliners, as Tizian is. You'll find the latest designs by international names, such as Rossi, Tods, Joop and Armani, which attract a rather *schickimicki* (smart and conservative) clientele.

Walter Steiger

**Schlüterstraße, 48
(map I, C3)
☎ 88 68 00 68**

Mon.-Fri. 10am-7pm,
Sat. 10am-4pm
U-Bahn Uhlandstraße.

If you're not a fashion victim,
yet not too closely wedded to
tradition either, you've come to
the right place. The pure white
interior of this shop, with its
subtle, filtered lighting, has
clearly been designed to focus
attention on the shoes. Walter
Steiger creates highly wearable
shoes for both and evening, with
prices around DM600. Stylish
sandals, slender court shoes and
smart high heels in black, pearl
grey and cream for lovers of
elegant footwear.

Bagage

**Bergmannstraße, 13
(map III, D1)
☎ 693 98 16
Mon.-Fri. 11am-8pm,
Sat. 10am-4pm
U-Bahn Gneisenaustraße.**

More bags than you could ever
use! From the old yellow leather
postman's bag recycled as a
handbag (a must in Berlin) to
travel bags and American
rucksacks, whatever your favourite
style, colour and material, it'll be
here. Customers range from ladies
of leisure to businessmen in a
hurry: they all know they'll find
just what they're looking for.

Tessuti

**Kurfürstendamm, 61
(map I, B3)
☎ 88 55 42 80
Mon.-Fri. 10am-7pm,
Sat. 10am-4pm
U-Bahn Adenauer Platz.**

Whether you're a budding fashion
designer or a home dressmaker,
this fabric shop is one of the best
in Berlin. Every fabric has its
own appeal, from the moiré
reflections of real silk to the
softness of cashmere. And if
you know how many metres/
yards you need to have one made
up, why not go for a linen suit or
jacket? This shop has built up
such a reputation that even people
from theatre and cinema
wardrobe departments come
here to stock up.

Fusion

**Heckmann Höfe (map II, C1)
Oranienburger Straße, 32
☎ 28 38 46 83
Tue.-Fri. 11am-8pm,
Sat. 11am-6pm
U-Bahn Oranienburger Straße.**

You won't find any junk jewellery
here. Ensconsed in their workshop, the two young gold and
silversmiths use only precious
metals to produce their jewellery.
Taking inspiration from their
fascination with antiques, they're
equally fervent in their love of the
shape and texture of the raw
materials of jewellery. Their gold
or matt silver necklaces, earrings
and rings (DM1,000-3,000) are
made in a variety of styles, from
the delicate ovals to the more
severe square shapes.

MEN'S FASHION

If there's one rule for dressing in Berlin, it's that there are no rules! Berliners are open to the most diverse influences. From 'English gentleman' to 'underground DJ', there are a wide variety of styles to choose from and a wide variety of shops to buy them in. Why not try something completely different and take on a whole new persona?

Ipuri

Kurfürstendamm, 216 (map I, C3)
☎ 881 35 10
Mon.-Fri. 10am-8pm,
Sat. 10am-4pm
U-Bahn Uhlandstraße.

Both sporty and classic, this is the ideal collection for a city weekend. A perfect cut and top-quality fabrics in shades of camel, grey and navy guarantees a quiet elegance. If you're looking for something for spring or autumn, the cotton mixture three-quarter-length coat could be a good bet (DM350).

Zeppelin

Oranienburger Straße, 87 (map II, C-D1)
☎ 172 311 14 48
Mon.-Fri. 10am-8pm,
Sat. 10am-4pm
U-Bahn Hackescher Markt.

Respectmen

Neue Schönhauser Straße, 14 (map II, D1)
☎ 283 50 10
Mon.-Fri. noon-8pm,
Sat. 11am-4pm
U-Bahn Hackescher Markt.

The designers Dirk Seidel, Karin and Alfred Warburg have plenty of fashion experience between them. Each year, they offer new cuts that are closely in keeping with the latest trends. Whether they're made to measure or off the peg, the jackets (DM500) and suits (DM800) hang perfectly and come mainly in dark colours and flannel, so you can stay trendy without being loud.

Falke

Quartier 206 (map II, C2)
Friedrichstraße, 71
☎ 20 94 61 10
Mon.-Fri. 10am-8pm,
Sat. 10am-4pm
U-Bahn Französische Straße.

If you want to leave Berlin dressed from head to toe in clothes you've bought in the city, you've come to the right place. Hugo Boss-style black leather moccasins and lace-up shoes with thick soles (DM250), the smartest of light or dark suits, shirts and matching ties (DM130) guarantee you'll leave the shop dressed to kill – unless you prefer something more casual, that is.

Anyone ever tell you that you look exactly like Brad Pitt ? Pity, because everything from the blue-grey cotton and linen shirts (DM140) to the restrained Armani ties (DM130) on sale here could help increase the resemblance. In this casual-wear shop, so typical of Berlin, they understand that it takes a great deal of effort to create the nonchalant laid-back appearance.

Apartment

Neue Schönhauser Straße, 11
(map II, D1)
☎ 281 55 34
Mon.-Fri. noon-8pm,
Sat. noon-4pm
U-Bahn Hackescher
Markt.

If you'd planned to go to a club (WMF or Tresor perhaps?) but are short of a few accessories, don't worry – you'll find everything you need here to give yourself a makeover in any style, from 1970s to 21st century. With a choice of acrylic and nylon trousers and T-shirts worthy of the top Berlin DJs, it's a great place to come for clubwear and streetwear. Whether you're looking for techno or hip hop, you won't come away empty-handed.

Uli Knecht

Kurfüstendamm, 30
(map I, C3)
☎ 88 67 78 42
Mon.-Fri. 10am-8pm,
Sat. 10am-4pm
U-Bahn Uhlandstraße.

If you go in for the traditional English gentleman look, then this is the place for you. Once you're dressed in a tweed jacket (DM800), flannel trousers and a discreet checked shirt, you'll convey a mixture of British upper class style and Italian fibre. But don't let your newly acquired formality stop you enjoying the delights of Berlin nightlife.

HOME ON THE RANGE

As any other large city, Berlin has more than its fair share of specialist clothes shops. Why not indulge your fantasies?

Saloon, Boots and Stuff
Oranienburger Straße 4
(map II, C-D1)
☎ 6 12 54 76
U-Bahn
Hackescher
Markt.

Just the place to purchase a flashy pair of cowboy boots, fringed shirt or bootlace tie, in fact everything you'll need to impress the ladies when you're line-dancing!

Patrick Hellmann

Fasanenstraße, 29
(map I, C3)
☎ 88 48 77 71
Mon.-Fri. 10am-7pm,
Sat. 9.30am-4pm
U-Bahn Uhlandstraße.

Whether they're made to measure or ready-to-wear designs by names such as Armani, Cerruti, Kiton and Calvin Klein, the suits (DM800-1000), blazers and shirts (DM150-200) in this shop are all very stylish. The district is home to lawyers and art dealers, and prices tend to reflect their high incomes, but in view of the service and quality on offer, it would be churlish to mention money.

Mila Camicie

Kurfüstendamm, 61
(map I, B3)
☎ 885 54 280
Mon.-Fri. 10am-7pm,
Sat. 10am-4pm
U-Bahn Adenauer Platz.

There are so many Italian shirts here you don't know which way to look! With its two distinct ranges, this shop has something for everyone. One range features classic, good-quality heavy cottons and is more for businessmen than party animals. The second line, sometimes bordering on the outrageous, is for those who like linen and silk decorated with floral and animal designs.

CHILDREN'S CLOTHES AND TOYS

Although Germany hasn't been spared the wave of electronic games that has swept the world, more traditional forms of entertainment now seem to be gaining ground. Make your visit to Berlin a chance to treat your children to wooden toys, marionnettes or construction kits. They'll develop all their senses and it will help them to learn while they play.

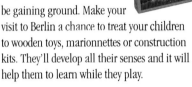

Tabularium

Große Hamburger Straße, 28 (map II, C1)
☎ 280 82 03
Mon.-Fri. 10.30am-8pm, Sat. 11am-7pm, Sun. 1-7pm
U-Bahn Hackescher Markt.

A stone's throw from Berlin's brand-new Jewish school, this shop is pleasing evidence of the rebirth of the district. While the bookshop clearly displays its cultural and religious orientation with numerous accounts of the history, culture and heritage of the German Jews, the toys and games section has a much wider appeal. As well as the chess sets, there are construction kits of the 'architectural monuments of the world' (DM150) to test your patience. Imagine trying to build the Taj Mahal or American Congress out of bricks!

Punkt und Pünktchen

Schlüterstraße, 28 (map I, C2-3)
☎ 324 78 90
Mon.-Fri. 10am-1pm, 3-6pm, Sat. 10am-2pm
U-Bahn Savignyplatz.

This shop makes life simpler for expectant mothers by displaying children's clothes alongside the maternity wear. Whether you're thinking of the present or the future, you're sure to find something you like here among all the sleepsuits, sailor suits and colour-coordinated outfits.

Vom Winde Verweht

Eisenacher Straße, 81 (map II, B1-2)
☎ 787 036 36
Mon.-Fri. 10am-1pm, 2.30-6.30pm, Sat. 10am-2pm
U-Bahn Eisenacher Straße.

As the name of this shop suggests ('Gone With the Wind') you're now in the realm of the acrobats of the sky, the rivals of Aeolus, Greek god of the wind. You'll find kites of all sizes for both amateurs and professionals and, more generally, everything that can be driven by the invisible force of the wind. Those who want to build their own kites and design everything down to their shape can get all the materials they need here, along with helpful advice.

Spielen Berlin

eue Schönhauser
traße, 8
map II, D1)
℡ 281 71 83
on.-Fri. 9.30am-7pm,
at. 9.30am-3pm
-Bahn Hackescher Markt.

ielen Berlin is the home of
ditional toys – there are no
ectronic games here, and very
le that relies on electricity, only
e rhythmic movement of the
cking horses and the clever
rking of the marionnette
ings. It's a nostalgic place where
ys and girls can happily play
h the kind of toys that their
ents loved and cherished.

mma & Co.

ebuhrstraße, 1
ap I, B-C3)
℡ 882 73 73
on.-Fri. 11am-6.30pm,
t. 11am-4pm
Bahn Savignyplatz.

the splendid setting of a
arlottenburg villa, the
erior of this shop is as
y as can be. On one side
re is the grown-ups'
artment, with its
tic furniture, and
lecloths and
ics in natural
ours; on the
er side
he villa is
area devoted to
dhood. To make your
pring look either streetwise
raditional, all you have to
s choose between the denim
garees and the Tyrolean
ket. And don't forget to buy
arming little wooden cart
hey can take their teddies
a ride.

Klein-Holz

Belziger Straße, 26
(map III, B2)
℡ 781 10 88
Mon.-Fri. 10am-6pm,
Sat. 10am-1.30pm
U-Bahn Eisenacher Straße.

If you're looking for something
educational, you can't beat
wooden toys. From construction
kits and games of skill to cranes,
lorries, boats and rocking horses
in natural colours, everything
here is made of solid wood.
Since
1982, the
association
has donated part of its profits to
the rehabilitation of young drug
addicts. If you buy a unique gift
here you'll be donating to a good
cause as well.

Spielbrett

Körtestraße, 27 (off map)
℡ 692 42 50
Mon.-Fri. 10am-6.30pm,
Sat. 10am-2pm
U-Bahn Schönleinstraße.

In a determined bid to slow
the irresistible rise in popularity
of electronic and computer
games, Spielbrett decided to
devote itself exclusively to the
sale of parlour games. They're
happy to advise you on your
choice of game, whether its a
fantasy game set in the time of
the Vikings or a strategic battle
game based on the Second
World War. As an added bonus,
they also organise games
evenings on a regular basis.

Zauberkönig

Hermannstraße,
84-90 (off map)
℡ 621 40 82
Mon.-Fri.
10am-6pm,
Sat. 11am-4pm
U-Bahn Leinestraße.

Anyone who's ever
dreamt of becoming
Merlin the Wizard or
joining the magic circle of
magicians would be well advised
to pay a visit to this mysterious
shop. From a magic wand to boxes
with false bottoms, more and
more tricks are revealed as you
dare to explore – to the great
displeasure of established
magicians everywhere.

DEPARTMENT STORES AND SHOPPING MALLS

The wave of American-style shopping malls, all with identical chains of shops, has reached Berlin and is still on the increase. However, alongside these predictable places, with their seething Saturday crowds, there are trendy, elegant new shops that will undoubtedly catch your eye. Contemporary architecture sometimes adds to their appeal, making them seem even more exclusive and shopping even more of a pleasure.

home, there are plenty of high-quality antique dealers. At Out of Asia the wood and the saffron-coloured fabrics seem to combine so well together that the only things that might stop you quenching your thirst for oriental decoration and furnishings are the prices. In winter you'll probably want to take advantage of the warmth of the underground gallery to reach Galeries Lafayette or Quartier 205.

are classified, not only according to composer, but also performer or conductor. If Cuban or Brazilian rhythms are more to your taste, make your way to the world music department, where you'll find sounds from just about every country. When it comes to the book department, a lot depends on how good your German is.

Quartier 206

Friedrichstraße, 71
(map II, C2)
☎ 20 94 62 76
Mon.-Fri. 10am-8pm,
Sat. 10am-4pm
U-Bahn Französische Straße.

Behind its façade of glass rectangles, which is illuminated at night, lies all the luxury of the new Berlin. Quartier 206 sets out to be majestic. You walk on marble pavements covered by a gigantic glass roof. On the fashion side, Gucci, Donna Karan and Etro set the tone. For the

Dussmann-Kulturkaufhaus

Friedrichstraße, 90
(map II, C1)
☎ 20 25 20 59
Mon.-Sat. 10am-10pm
U-Bahn Friedrichstraße.

The mecca of cultural consumption, Dussmann is a great success in the Berlin marketplace. With its unusually long opening hours, this large book and record store aims to put customer service first. If you pride yourself on being a discerning music lover, pay a visit to the basement, where the classical CDs and records

Galeries Lafayette

Friedrichstraße, 76
(map II, C2)
☎ 20 94 80
Mon.-Fri. 9.30am-8pm,
Sat. 9am-4pm
U-Bahn Französische Straß

here's glass everywhere you
ook in this distinctive building
esigned by Jean Nouvel.
urrounded in places by
affolding, to protect passers-by
om the dangers of a
uilding that has been
eakened by the wind, the
hop was designed around a
umber of glass cones and
e architecture is so
npressive that you
n't help wondering
hether the crowds
ome here to admire
e design or to shop.
airly small branch
the famous
arisian department
re, a visit to the
od halls, with their
e wines and good-
ality fast foods,
a must. The fashion
partments stock
the famous
ternational brand
mes and the
re is chock-full
beautiful but
newhat expensive
ms.

aufhaus
ertheim

rfürstendamm 231
ap I, C3)
88 00 30
n.-Fri. 10am-8pm,
t. 10am-4pm
Bahn Kurfürstendamm.

e successor to the house of
rtheim, this store was

originally founded
in Leipziger Straße in
1905 and maintains
a long tradition of
retailing that was
brutally interrupted by
the war. Now located in the
Ku'damm, in the heart of
the Charlottenburg shopping
district, its modern flagship
store has four floors devoted to
the latest trends and big names
of international fashion for
both men and women; interior
decoration and designer
tableware collections are also
strongly represented.

Potsdamer Platz
Arkaden

Potsdamer Platz
(map II, B2)
Mon.-Sat. 9am-8pm
U-Bahn Potsdamer Platz.

There's no denying the American
influence on the city, underlined
by huge shopping malls that have
sprung up like this one. Designed
by Italian architect Renzo
Piano, over a hundred highly
standardised shops, restaurants

and bars fill the three floors of
the pedestrian shopping precinct.
It's constantly full to brimming
with crowds of recently arrived
businessmen and Berliners

happy to be able to find
everything they want under one
enormous glass roof. Big
international names, such as
Hennes & Mauritz, Falke and
Mango sit side by side with
the many small restaurants
specialising in Turkish, Chinese
and Italian food.

INTERIOR DECORATION, TABLEWARE AND DESIGN

While the well-known designers of Northern Europe are still in evidence, a new generation of young Berlin designers has recently emerged. An attraction for the great classics, a passion for Mediterranean influences and a strong dose of Germanic common sense mingle together producing exciting designs that are both beautiful and practical.

Glasklar

**Knesebeckstraße, 13-14
(map I, C2)
☎ 313 10 37
Mon.-Sat. 11am-6.30pm
U-Bahn Ernst-Reuter-Platz.**

Whether you want brandy, whisky, liqueur or wine glasses, with or without stems, they come in so many different shapes and sizes here that it's almost impossible to make a choice. The same is true of their vases, too, and given the very reasonable prices (from DM1 a glass), you can forget about matching sets and simply buy whatever you please.

Küchenladen

**Knesebeckstraße, 26
(map I, C2)
☎ 881 39 08
Mon.-Fri. 10am-7pm,
Sat. 10am-4pm
U-Bahn Savignyplatz.**

You may not have come away for the weekend with the idea of returning with a set of saucepans, but there'll always be keen cooks somewhere who can't wait to get something simmering on the stove as soon as they get home. You can rest assured, Germany may not be the home of gastronomy, but it can certainly lay claim to being the home of culinary technology. Judge for yourself – melon knives, made-to-measure utensils and electric gadgets of every kind are sold alongside the books containing the recipes they help you to cook. You can't say better than that!

Rahaus

**Nürnberger Straße, 50
(map I, D3)
☎ 217 70 06
Mon.-Fri. 11am-8pm,
Sat. 10am-4pm
U-Bahn Wittenbergplatz.**

You won't bring back anything truly unique from this home decoration, furnishing and gadget supermarket, but as you browse the shelves, the translucent red, blue or green soapdishes (DM5), eggcups in the form of royal crowns (DM3) or brightly-coloured table mats (DM6) may catch your eye and bring to mind the shapes and colours of the tea set you had as a child.

Station Nord

**Auguststraße, 28 (map II, C
☎ 283 90 606
Tue.-Fri. 11am-6pm,
Sat. noon-4pm
U-Bahn Hackescher Markt**

As its name suggests, this shop is home to Scandinavian furniture and home decor designs. In the fifties, the celebrated Alvar Aalto graced Berlin with several of his architectural creations, but the present day belongs to his pupils and those who are carrying on his work. All the more reason to admire the ew styles and materials regularly isplayed in this shop. For those who are put off by the stark implicity of the furniture, there re colourful carpets or unusual rnaments, glassware and lamps DM250).

Karthago

'estalozzistraße, 105
map I, C2)
☎ 806 04 803
Mon.-Fri. 10am-8pm,
at. 10am-4pm
-Bahn Savignyplatz.

n't miss the opportunity to
ring back a little of the splendour
the Middle East. The rich
rpets, ceremonial knives, low
rniture and wall hangings from
amascus and Marrakesh
come with a certificate
authenticity.

Jeanne Koepp

Kollwitzstraße, 53
(off map)
☎ 441 95 91
Tue.-Fri. 1-7pm,
Sat. noon-4pm
U-Bahn Senderfelderplatz.

Jeanne Koepp, who
shares her ceramics
workshop with a
goldsmith, mixes
colours and
materials to
stunning effect.
Her mixture
of bright red and
enamels so closely
resembles Chinese ceramic art
that you can't help suspecting
that she got the recipe directly
from them. While the workshop
has two separate parts, with each
artist reigning supreme in her
own area, the arrangement allows
each of them to influence the
creative endeavours of the other.

Lichthaus Mösch

Tauentzienstraße, 7a
(map I, D3)
☎ 214 86 30
Mon.-Fri. 10am-8pm,
Sat. 10am-4pm
U-Bahn Wittenbergplatz.

On the two floors of this lighting
warehouse, you'll find everything
you've ever dreamt of in the way
of lighting – lamps to
light the darkest
corner or largest

room, to read by as you lie on a
sofa, to illuminate your keyboard
at your computer desk or to put
your favourite painting in a
favourable light.

A word of
advice before you rush along to
the shop – try and have some
idea of the style and colour
you're looking for. Then you'll
be able to make your choice
without the risk of being quite
so dazzled!

Up Arts

Goltzstraße, 12 (map III, B1)
☎ 216 90 21
Mon.-Fri. 11am-7pm,
Sat. 11am-4pm
U-Bahn Nollendorfplatz.

TON IN TON

Mommsenstraße, 3
(map I, B-C3)
☎ 881 32 17
Mon.-Fri. 11am-7pm,
Sat. 11am-2pm
U-Bahn Savignyplatz.

Just because the shop is so
narrow doesn't mean it
isn't worth taking a look
inside – you won't be
disappointed. At first sight,
it's difficult to say
whether these original
ceramics owe more
to Mediterranean
influences or abstract
works of art by
Kandinsky. Large
platters, small dishes and
vases in earthy tones are
available from DM150.

Berg, mixes various neutral shades with splashes of bright citrus colours to achieve exciting effects in his furniture designs. You may not usually like strong contrasts and prefer to avoid anything too pretentious, but you should really take a look in this shop. You may surprise yourself and come out with a spiral coffee table or even an unstructured desk.

If you're seeking spirituality, you're more than likely to find something to interest you among 'Up Arts' interesting selection of African amulets, ritual masks from Papua-New Guinea and Buddhist statues from Tibet – though you may well feel safer with a votive statue that's designed to ward off evil spirits.

time refined. Neither too utilitarian nor simply gadgets, the objects on sale here will harmonise with your home, whatever the decor. It's the ideal place to come if you're thinking of brightening up your bathroom or livening up your kitchen. The prices are moderate and the sales assistants charming, so why hesitate?

Filiala

Winterfeldstraße, 42
(map III, B1)
☎ 215 74 75
Mon.-Fri. 10am-8pm,
Sat. 9am-4pm
U-Bahn Nollendorfplatz.

Avoiding ostentation, Filiala advocates a style of design that's trendy but at the same

Bella Form

Wörther Straße, 32
(off map)
☎ 44 00 92 62
Tue.-Fri. noon-8pm,
Sat. 11am-4pm
U-Bahn Senefelderplatz.

This interior designer with a shop near Kollwitzplatz, the nerve centre of trendy Prenzlauer

Arno

S-Bahnbögen-Savignyplatz
(map I, C3)
☎ 315 94 90
Mon.-Fri. 10am-8pm,
Sat. 10am-4pm
U-Bahn Savignyplatz.

Established in 1927, this shop under the S-Bahn arches has cultivated a tradition of quality and has become something of an authority on interior design. If you have the means and the desire, there's nothing to stop you giving your home a complete makeover. Everything here lends itself to it, from the amazing fluid sculptures that act as lamps (DM300-400), to fabulous desks that could almost make you want to work at the week-end.

GALERIE SPLINTER

Sophie-Gips-Höfe
(map II, C1)
Sophienstraße, 20-21
☎ 28 59 87 37
Tue.-Fri. 2-7pm,
Sat. 11am-6pm
U-Bahn Weinmeisterstraße.

New creations and antique glass pieces are displayed here side by side, as if to show that a secret link that unites them across time. The entire basement space of the gallery

given over to a display of the glassware, with one-offs from DM50) and original signs by international designers. From the massive abstract sculptures to the intricate designs of hand-own glass pieces, the accent on the fluidity of a noble material.

Modus

Kurlandstraße, 28
(map I, B3)
☎ 882 73 81
Mon.-Fri. 10am-6.30pm,
10am-4pm
U-Bahn Savignyplatz.

Modus has already acquired something of a reputation in Berlin, having entirely redecorated interior of the Rotes Rathaus, 'red town hall'. It's an understatement to say that they're proud to show you that the great designers are quite at home here. From the objects by Le Corbusier those by Achille Castelogni, to Bill and Philippe Starck, it's the once avant-garde, now classic designs, that are on show here.

Stue

Alte Schönhauser
Straße, 48 (map II, D1)
☎ 247 276 50
Mon.-Fri. noon-7pm,
Sat. noon-4pm
U-Bahn
Weinmeisterstraße.

If you feel nostalgic at the mere mention of the 1970s, then this is definitely the shop for you. Set out like a show apartment, it has a series of rooms leading from the entrance hall through to the sitting room, only missing out on the kitchen. The objects and pieces of furniture come to life in their natural settings, whether they're natural wood tables, wall units, leather armchairs or ceiling lights.

Habitare

Savignyplatz, 7-8 (map I, C3)
☎ 31 86 47 11
Mon.-Fri. 10am-8pm,
Sat. 10am-4pm
U-Bahn Savignyplatz.

Natural wood chairs, teak benches, bistro tables and brightly coloured kilims set the tone and show that Berlin has opened its doors to Mediterranean influences. From the café terraces opening on every street, the blossoming Italian restaurants and the convertibles cruising the roads outside the shop, it would appear that the lifestyle it's advocating certainly has its followers.

Rooms Interior

Winterfeldtstraße, 46
(map III, B1)
☎ 21 75 41 12
Mon.-Fri. 10am-8pm,
Sat. 9am-4pm
U-Bahn Nollendorfplatz.

You'll find a whole range of easily portable objects here that are somewhere between a Japanese influence and the major trends of international design. For the kitchen, you may be attracted by the generous bowls or perhaps the little rectangular dishes that can used as serving plates for sushi or as ashtrays on the coffee table in the sitting-room. In other words, it's a good place to come if you're looking for those last-minute presents to take back.

ANTIQUE SHOPS AND FLEA MARKETS

Renowned for Art Nouveau, Art Deco and the many influences left behind by the Bauhaus, Berlin is the haunt of a multitude of secondhand dealers and flea markets *(Trödel und Flohmarkt)*, where the best and the worst work side by side. If bargain-hunting doesn't appeal and the avant-garde is out of the question, you can always invest in a centuries-old Biedermeier antique.

Werner Keller

**Solmstraße, 36
(map III, D1)
☎ 692 31 42
Mon.-Fri.
2-6.30pm
U-Bahn
Gneisenaustraße.**

The jumble of objects on display in this shop may look like mere bric-a-brac but it's worth examining more closely. However, it's best to have a clear idea of the aesthetic legacy of 20th-century design before you come, if you don't want your friends to laugh when they see the bright orange lamp or brown plastic armchair you just couldn't resist buying!

Trödel- und Kunstmarkt

**Straße der 17-Juli
(map I, C-D2)
☎ 26 55 00 96
Sat.-Sun. 10am-5pm
U-Bahn Tiergarten.**

Some people say it's a tourist trap, but the fact remains that, just a stone's throw from the

Tiergarten, the most famous flea market in Berlin still retains its charm. You may not find the antique of your dreams here, but if you ferret about in the boxes of books, old postcards and engravings, you may be attracted to some souvenir of turn-of-the-century Berlin. Then again you may prefer the uniforms and *shapkas* (hats) of the Warsaw Pact, though it's usually the handmade hemp and cotton clothes that catch the eye of bargain-hunters – it's all a question of taste.

Flohmarkt

**Am Kupfergraben
(map II, C1)
Sat.-Sun. 10am-5pm
U-Bahn Friedrichstraße.**

Along the Spree and the Museuminsel, between the Pergamon and the Bode Museum, the riverbank is covered every weekend with stalls with a hint of nostalgia. It has more the feel of a church fete or a jumble sale than a flea market. The family silver, GDR literature, leather jackets and coats straight out of spy films all help to keep alive the memory of a past that's still all too present in people's minds.

Flohmarkt am Arkonaplatz

**Arkonaplatz (off map)
☎ 93 79 87 55
Sun. 10am-5pm
U-Bahn Bernauer Straße.**

Wild 1950s to 1970s design appears to be the last word in

Berlin chic, so what could be more natural than for the leading exponent of the style to have set up shop in the heart of Prenzlauer Berg? Some people will say it's out of sync, others will say it's quite crazy. After indulging in one of the copious Frühstücksbuffets of the district on a Sunday morning, it's a pleasure to stroll between the formica tables and clothes rails covered with enough flowery outfits to please any ABBA fan.

Antiquitäten am Scheunenviertel

Tucholskystraße, 37
(map II, C1)
☎ 283 53 53
Tue.-Fri. 2-6.30pm,
Sat. noon-4pm
U-Bahn Oranienburger Straße.

At last some traditional old Biedermeier antiques! Amongst the small mahogany cigar boxes and burr elm liqueur chests, all the social necessities of the 19th-century middle-class German are looking for a home here. The well-tended shop also sells desks

and card tables that are so highly polished you can see your reflection in them. Worth a look, even if you come away empty-handed.

China Antik

Auguststraße, 28 (map II, C1)
☎ 28 38 44 05
Tue.-Fri. 3-7pm,
Sat. noon-4pm
U-Bahn Oranienburger Straße.

The fashion for oriental art has reached Berlin, along with so many other European capitals,

so what could be more natural than to find the trend reflected among the antique dealers? If you're looking for the genuine article, you'll be tempted by the furniture from northern China displayed here. All the pieces are guaranteed restored and re-lacquered on the premises, only the deep colour of their woods bear witness to their former lives.

Galerie Hans-Peter Jochum

Bleibtreustraße, 41
(map I, C3)
☎ 882 16 12
Mon.-Fri. 2-6.30pm,
Sat. 11am-2pm
U-Bahn Savignyplatz.

The parquet flooring, white walls, shelves bearing armchairs (DM2,000-3,000), chairs and stools all serve as reminders that the Bauhaus designers and their heirs were intent on purity and

simplicity of form. In this establishment, which is somewhere between a gallery and an antique shop, you're among art connoisseurs, and it shows.

Lehmanns Colonialwaren

Grolmanstraße, 46
(map I, C2-3)
☎ 883 39 42
Tue.-Fri. 2-7pm,
Sat. 11am-2pm
U-Bahn Savignyplatz.

If you're nostalgic for the age of empires, and dream of far-flung lands with evocative names, this shop will bring your childhood fantasies to life. From the models of old sailing ships and the globes that are enough to make any budding explorer sigh with longing, to the leather suitcases and trunks that travellers once covered in stickers to show the countries they'd visited on their voyages, everything here will remind you of a colonial past.

SECONDHAND SHOPS

In spite of its new status as the capital of Germany, Berlin remains first and foremost the capital of make do and mend – so why consign old household objects of the GDR, 1970s designs and your granny's clothes to the attic? At a time when every object can be recycled at least two or three times, you can make a virtue of necessity and have some fun as well.

Rock Steady Rec.

Maaßenstraße, 5
(map III, B1)
☎ 217 27 20
Mon.-Fri. 11am-7pm,
Sat. 10am-4pm
U-Bahn Nollendorfplatz.

If you want to add a few rare items to your record collection or simply start a new one, this place is worth a visit. Whatever your taste in music – soul, rock, hip hop or techno – you're sure to find something to treasure among the old vinyl records and huge number of CDs on offer, all at unbeatable prices (DM1-15).

Schönhauser

Neue Schönhauser Straße, 18
(map II, D1)
☎ 281 17 04
Mon.-Fri. noon-8pm,
Sat. 11am-4pm
U-Bahn Hackescher Markt.

Plastic furniture, Leatherette armchairs, orange globes that shed a characteristic light – everything reminiscent of 1970s style is back in force in trendy Berlin, sometimes at almost indecent prices. This shop is no exception to the rule and it's worth paying special attention to the objects most representative of the former GDR, such as the electric toasters and other kitchen equipment.

Kleidermarkt Garage

Ahornstraße, 2
(map III, B1)
☎ 211 27 60
Mon.-Wed. 11am-7pm,
Thu.-Fri. 11am-8pm,
Sat. 10am-4pm
U-Bahn Nollendorfplatz.

second hand shop

This secondhand clothes market, where the clothes are sold by weight (DM25.95/kg/2.2lb), is mainly frequented by casual young Berliners, who come here to pass the time as much as to hunt for bargains. Although there's an enormous choice of clothes on offer, you're more likely to find an outfit for clubbing than an evening dress to wear to the opera.

Kleidermarkt Colours

**Bergmannstraße, 102
(map III, D1)
☎ 694 33 48
Mon.-Wed. 11am-7pm,
Thu.-Fri. 11am-8pm,
Sat. 10am-4pm
U-Bahn Gneisenaustraße.**

Most of the clothes you'll find here come straight from the United States and date from the 1970s and 1980s. Which means that if you want to visit Kreuzberg incognito, dressed as an alternative rebel, a quick trip to this shop is a must. From the techno T-shirt (DM10) to the trench coat (DM100), you'll be spoilt for choice for something to wear to fit in with the atmosphere of the district.

Calypso

**Münzstraße, 16 (map II, D1)
☎ 281 61 65
Mon.-Fri. noon-8pm,
Sat. noon-4pm
U-Bahn Weinmeisterstraße.**

If you turn a blind eye to the chaos and bravely step inside this shop, you'll find yourself in the home of secondhand shoes. It may look like a theatrical costumiers or props shop but its actually the best-stocked shoe-shop in the city. With cowboy boots, biker boots, Doc Martens and moccasins, as well as stilettos and thigh boots of yesteryear on offer, you can take on any persona you please.

Macy's

**Kommsenstraße, 2
(map I, B-C3)
☎ 881 13 63
Mon.-Fri. 11am-6.30pm,
Sat. 11am-4pm
U-Bahn Uhlandstraße.**

If you love wearing designer clothes, but like to stand out from the crowd, you'll feel quite at home here. At Macy's you'll find clothes by Armani, Jil Sander, Versace and Prada, all at knock-down prices. They may, of course, date from a few seasons back and have had other owners but that doesn't stop them being a good buy, and at least you can be stylish without looking a victim of fashion.

Mega Dress

**Goltzstraße, 13
(map III, B1)
☎ 216 55 88
Mon.-Fri. noon-6pm,
Sat. 11am-2pm
U-Bahn Nollendorfplatz.**

When you leave this trendy, retro shop you'll be wearing bright colours rather than the usual safe black. In a very kitsch setting, the most unexpected secondhand clothes can be found alongside the more standard items. Don't come thinking you'll leave kitted out from head to foot, the main thing on offer is the atmosphere.

STERLING GOLD

**Heckmann Höfe
(map III, C1)
Oranienburger Straße, 32
☎ 611 32 17
Mon.-Fri. noon-8pm,
Sat. 11am-4pm
U-Bahn Oranienburger
Straße.**

You don't need the excuse of a fancy-dress party to dress up in smart 1950s, 1960s or 1970s gear. Here you'll find an impressive selection of evening dresses and outfits for that special occasion. From candy pink and snow white to royal blue and black, they're arranged according to their colour. For a reasonable price (DM120-350), you'll be able to turn yourself into 'eine Berlinerin' for the space of an evening, and be the belle of the ball.

SPORT

Having been the object of as much political as sporting conflagration during the 1936 Olympic Games, and an unsuccessful candidate for those in 2000, Berlin is now bidding to host the football World Cup finals in 2006. Putting the politics of sport aside, try exploring the city on a motorbike or roller skates and if you have all the right equipment, you can go for a hike in the Brandenburg countryside as well.

Niketown

Tauentzienstraße
(map I, D3)
☎ 25 07 0
Mon.-Fri. 10am-8pm,
Sat. 10am-4pm
U-Bahn
Wittenbergplatz.

Nike has opened a store in Berlin before London! All the more reason to come here to discover the latest trends and new textiles. With its ultramodern layout organised around the major sporting activities, Niketown allows you to spot at a glance the basic shoes and equipment you need for a particular sport as you wander from one area to another surrounded by posters glorifying the athletes sponsored by the brand.

360°

Pariser Straße, 24
(map I, B3)
☎ 883 85 96
Mon.-Fri. 11am-7.30pm,
Sat. 10am-4pm
U-Bahn Adenauer Platz.

This is definitely *the* place to come for all your skateboarding, snowboarding, skiing, surfing and windsurfing equipment. Whatever your sport, you sure to be amazed by the choice of shapes and designs on offer. And if extreme sport will always stay a fantasy for you, you can still dress the part, with surf shorts, baggy khaki trousers with wide pockets, a trendy rucksack (DM50-150) and stylishly cool sunglasses.

Mont Klamott

Kastanienallee, 83 (off map)
☎ 448 25 90
Mon.-Fri. 10am-8pm,
Sat. 10am-4pm
U-Bahn Eberswalder Straße.

The Brandenburg area doesn't really lend itself to trekking but, midway between the Alps and the Scandinavian North, Berlin serves as a starting point for large numbers of adventurers. If you're one of them, you won't come away empty-handed. On the two floors of this shop, an army of assistants will do their very best to help you find your way through the maze of rucksacks, sleeping bags and climbing equipment. As a bonus, they'll give you valuable advice about hiking in nearby Sächsische Schweiz and Märkische Schweiz.

Karstadt Sport

Joachimstaler Straße, 5-6
(map 1, C2-3)
☎ 880 240
Mon.-Fri. 10am-8pm,
Sat. 9am-4pm
U-Bahn Zoologischer Garten.

The biggest sports department
store in Berlin is an Aladdin's
Cave for all sporty types. Take
advantage of this supermarket
to bring your equipment up to
date. For the first-time visitor, the
aim of the game is either to go
straight to the department of your
favourite sport or to patiently
try to track down the sporting
activity that *isn't* represented.

OLYMPIASTADION

Olympischer Platz
(off map)
☎ 300 63-3
Every day, 9am-sunset
Entry charge
U-Bahn Olympiastadion
(Ost).

Designed by Werner March
for the 1936 Olympics, the
Olympic stadium is the only
example of Nazi architecture
to survive intact in Berlin. The
place still resounds to the feats
of the black American athlete
Jesse Owens, winner of four
gold medals, who stood up to
Nazi racism and made Hitler's
supremist theories look
ridiculous. Now the home
ground of the Berlin football
club Herta BSC, the
75,000 capacity
stadium dreams of
hosting the 2006
World Cup.

Harley Davidson Motorclothes

Lietzenburger Straße, 90
(map 1, C3)
☎ 882 49 15
Mon.-Fri. 10am-6.30pm,
Sat. 10am-2pm
U-Bahn Uhlandstraße.

Berlin is so vast, that it's an
ideal place to tour on a Harley
Davidson, with the engine
throbbing and your hair blowing
in the wind. If you love the
bikes and have a licence,
you can hire one of these
mechanical monsters for the
day (DM150-230 according to
model). Biking enthusiasts can
get all the necessary accessories
here – T-shirts bearing the
logo of the legendary make,
leather suits, boots and gloves.

Strawberry

Emser Straße, 45 (off map)
☎ 881 30 96
Mon.-Fri. 11am-8pm,
Sat.-Sun. 11am-4pm
U-Bahn Hohenzollernplatz.

If you fancy a truely original
way of discovering Berlin, why
not try roller blades? This shop
will hire you a pair of roller
blades for the day (DM15) or
weekend (DM25), and they'll
also suggest an interesting route
for you to take. Don't worry if
you haven't got anything suitable
to wear – the shop specialises in
women's streetwear.

Eisdieler

Kastanienallee, 12 (off map)
☎ 28 57 35
Mon.-Fri. noon-8pm,
Sat. noon-6pm
U-Bahn Eberswalderstraße.

The name of this shop has
long been a jealously guarded
secret passed from mouth to
mouth by members of the young,
trendy Berlin scene. Four young
designers, Stefan, Ove, Olaf and
Till, were responsible for its
opening in 1994 and it has since
developed its own streetwear,
clubwear and sportswear labels.
From the simple basic accessories
(DM50) to the Goretex jacket,
you'll find everything the modern
adventurer needs to get by in
the city jungle.

GOURMET DELIGHTS

While it may not boast as many famous gourmet delights as some other European countries, Germany, especially Berlin, has always been interested in the cuisines of the world. If you'd like to see what treats of its own Berlin has to offer, you'll find below some addresses that will act as a guide to the world of German culinary specialities.

Wald

**Pestalozzistraße, 54a
(map I, C2)
☎ 323 82 54
Mon.-Fri. 2-6pm,
Sat. 11am-4pm
U-Bahn Savignyplatz.**

Irmgard Wald's recipe for 'Königsberg' marzipan is a closely guarded secret, and she has been tirelessly producing her delectable speciality for fifty years. Rolled and pressed by hand, mixed with nougat and walnuts and sprinkled with liqueur, it's ready to pop into the oven. Only then, and with great ceremony, will you be allowed to sample its delights.

Operncafé im Opernpalais

**Unter den Linden, 5
(map II, C2)
☎ 20 26 83
Every day, 9am-midnight
U-Bahn Hausvogteiplatz.**

A paradise for lovers of old-fashioned cream cakes and tarts, this Viennese-style café a stone's throw from the opera, prides itself on offering the best pastries in the city. Whether you eat them on the spot or take them away to eat at home, they certainly live up to their reputation, at least if the queue in front of the counter is anything to go by.

Lutter & Wegner

**Charlottenstraße, 56
(map II, C2)
☎ 202 95 40
Every day, 11-2am
U-Bahn Stadtmitte.**

Apart from a few interruptions caused by Berlin's troubled past, this august establishment prides itself on having been in existence since 1811. Over the course of its long life it has served wine to a

number of famous people from Berlin's past, including E. T. A. Hoffmann and Adalbert von Chamisso. A wine cellar next to an Art Nouveau restaurant, you'll be able to taste some of the vintages of Franconia and the Rhineland-Palatinate until late at night, before you decide to export a few cases of it.

Hardy im Weinhaus Huth

**Alte Potsdamer Straße, 5
(map II, B2)
☎ 25 29 72 80
Mon.-Fri. 9.30am-8pm,
Sat. 9am-4pm
U-Bahn Potsdamer Platz.**

Confiserie Melanie

**Goethestraße, 4
(map I, B2)
☎ 313 83 30
Mon.-Fri. 10am-7pm,
Sat. 10am-2pm
U-Bahn Bismarckstraße.**

If you like mixtures of salt and sweet flavours and unusual taste combinations, you'll love Eberhard Päller's latest ideas. This confectioner shows he is willing to try anything. Be warned, he has chocolates flavoured with thyme, curry and garlic. Love them or hate them, you have to admit that they're original!

Fitzroy-Der Bioladen

**Großbeerenstraße 11
(map III, D1)
☎ 217 23 45
Mon.-Fri. 9am-6.30pm,
Sat. 9am-1pm
U-Bahn
Möckernbrücke.**

It's a mystery why they chose the famous rockface of Tierra del Fuego as their shop sign, but perhaps it was out of respect for the bounty of mother Earth. With the atmosphere of a country grocer's, this shop conceals many culinary delights. The company motto proclaims that the only healthy products are organic products and next to the inevitable wholemeal bread, you'll find a perfectly respectable little Kaiserstuhl wine.

This building is all that remains of the Potsdamer Platz of yesteryear. It was miraculously saved from the wave of destruction that followed the war, but was lost until recently in the middle of no-man's-land. An old wine and liqueur merchants, it has at last been restored to its original purpose amidst all the skyscrapers. Alongside the foreign wines, which are well represented here, the raspberry, pear and other fruit liqueurs (DM70-150) merit special attention, as do the wines of the Rhineland-Palatinate. If you ask for advice, you'll be invited to taste them.

Konstanza

**Konstanzer Straße, 10
(map I, B3)
☎ 881 34 28
Mon.-Fri. 9.30am-6.30pm,
Sat. 9am-2pm
U-Bahn Konstanzer
Straße.**

The Germans are well-versed in organic produce and this bright, pleasant, almost countrified establishment is the ideal place for you to try some. Apart from the obvious fruit and vegetables, you'll find delicious honey and many tempting German wines. The organic cosmetics on offer may be of interest to those with sensitive skins, so if you've never tried them, now's the time.

THE UNUSUAL AND THE BIZARRE

Every city has a hidden side, full of secret fantasies. Here, far from everyday reality, a bizarre world of alternative lives, outrageous clothes and cyberculture weaves an invisible web. After you've discovered and explored this disconcerting world, it would be a pity not to bring back a souvenir of your visit, however brief.

You don't need to be particularly devout to find the recipe for earthly happiness here: incense sticks, South American portable altars, items from monasteries all over Europe and a wide variety of other religious objects will take you on a whirlwind tour of faiths all around the world at very little cost.

C-base

**Oranienburger Straße, 2
(map II, C1)
☎ 28 59 93 00
According to events,
from 3pm to 4.30am
U-Bahn Hackescher
Markt.**

At the end of a courtyard, you'll find an enigmatic neon sign over a heavy iron door that opens to reveal a bizarre, futuristic world. It looks and feels like a spaceship and has been built out of an assortment of scrap aeronautical equipment by a group of young Berliners, who organise electronic games tournaments, Internet nights and photo exhibitions here. There's no regular programme of events, but you should do your utmost to get on board the space station!

Ave Maria & Devotionalien

**Potsdamer Straße, 75
(map II, B3)
☎ 262 12 11
Mon.-Fri. noon-7pm,
Sat. noon-3pm
U-Bahn Kurfürstenstraße.**

Kaufhaus Schrill

**Bleibtreustraße, 46
(map I, C3)
☎ 882 40 48
Mon.-Fri. 11am-7pm,
Sat. 10am-4pm
U-Bahn Savignyplatz.**

You could say this shop's a real drag! From the bright, colourful wigs that are worn in the Love Parade to imitation diamond necklaces and tiaras for Christopher Street Day, it has everything you could possibly want to create a simply divine drag queen outfit. All you have to do now is climb aboard the right float and you'll be ready for the parade.

Collectio Navalis

Goethestraße, 78
(map I, C2)
☎ 313 18 81
Tue.-Fri. 11am-6pm,
Sat. 10am-1pm
U-Bahn Savignyplatz.

If you've ever laid in the bath,
dreaming of sinking battleships,
then this is your chance to swap
your lead soldiers for model ships
and have a go at playing naval
battles! Liners, cruisers and
battleships wait patiently in this
shop for someone to bring them
to life. If this kind of game
doesn't appeal to you, you may
be interested in the tales of
maritime adventures or the old
naval documents (1914-1945),
nostalgic reminders of the days
of long sea voyages.

Transformation

Marburger Straße, 16
(map I, C3)
☎ 21 47 70 57
Mon.-Fri. 9am-8pm,
Sat. 9am-4pm
U-Bahn Kurfürstendamm.

If you fancy a change of sex
for the evening, these discreet
salons can make your dreams
and fantasies become a reality.
In four hours and for DM300,
you can be transformed into
a member of the opposite
sex. For an extra DM100,
they'll even make you into
a bride for the day.
However, if you'd
rather carry out the
transformation in
the privacy of your
own home, silicone
breasts, outrageous
wigs and high heeled
shoes in men's sizes
are also available.

Ufo-Phantastische Buchhandlung

Bergmannstraße, 25
(map III, D1)
☎ 69 50 51 17
U-Bahn Gneisenaustraße.

Whether you're a Spiderman
aficionado or a keen Star Trek
fan, this science fiction bookshop
will take you on a journey into
space. Its stock ranges from the
original American albums of
the 1940s and 1950s to the
most up-to-date examples of the
genre, including Star Wars.

If you're a natural sceptic and
still doubt the existence of extra-
terrestrial life, this shop
may make you change
your mind.

Aquarius Wassergalerie

Bleibtreustraße, 3
(map I, C3)
☎ 31 50 68 90
Mon.-Fri. 11am-
7.30pm,
Sat. 10am-4pm
U-Bahn Savignyplatz.

From fountains running
with perfume and musical
water jets to hydraulic
sprays (from DM70),
the more playful aspects
of water are transformed
into works of art in this
establishment.
Multi-coloured
sculptures have
water streaming
down them in
hidden channels.
Inspired by Eastern
philosophies and

Oranienburger Straße, 90
(map II, C1)
☎ 28 38 66 99
Mon.-Fri. 11am-7pm,
Sat. 10.30am-4pm
U-Bahn Hackescher Markt.

Once you're on the other side
of the mirror, you'll think
you've stumbled into Lewis
Carroll's Wonderland. There
are chests of drawers in a
variety of colours and strange
designs, including heart-shaped
and egg-shaped (from DM700),
and furniture from deepest
Africa to transport you to a
world that's both outrageous
and enchanting. These
creations by international
artists have the strength of the
dreams and nightmares of
childhood.

Japanese gardens, these water
columns (DM2,400) reflect the
harmonious elements of the
natural world.

MARKETS AND COVERED MARKETS

While Berlin is no Mediterranean city with market stalls on every street corner, it still has places worthy of interest, where Berliners like to stroll on Saturday mornings seeking out fresh produce to last them the week-end. Always different, always lively, both the markets and covered markets are often a good reflection of a district's spirit and history. Whether they sell local produce, colourful exotic delicacies, or gourmet delights, they will show you the amazing diversity of the city and its inhabitants.

'Türkenmarkt' am Maybachufer

Maybachufer (off map)
Tue. and Fri. noon-6.30pm
U-Bahn Schönleinstraße.

Although it's located in the Neukölln district, the Turkish market is closely connected with cosmopolitan Kreuzberg. In a provincial atmosphere on the left bank of the Landwehrkanal, whole families come here to find a little of their native Turkey. The fruit and vegetable stalls differ little from those in western markets, but the Turkish specialities (*falafel*, spices, brioche-like bread and pastries) are a good reason to come here. In any case, you come as much for the Mediterranean atmosphere as to fill your shopping basket. After this brief incursion into the everyday life of Berlin's Turkish community, cross to the other bank and allow yourself to be tempted by the southern cuisine at *Cucina Mediterranea*.

Winterfeldmarkt

Winterfeldplatz
(map III, B1)
Wed. and Sat. 8am-1pm
U-Bahn Nollendorfplatz.

For Berliners, this is certainly the most upmarket of the city's markets, a place you come to both for the pleasure of shopping and to meet people. In the heart of the Schöneberg district, it perpetuates a certain way of life and gives the square its charm. The ideal time to come here is on a Saturday, when young lovers and trendy parents wander from stall to stall looking for Canadian muffins, Italian and French cheese or *spreewalder Gurken*, impressive-looking gherkins with a multitude of seasonings and flavourings. It's best to get here early if you want to take advantage of the district's many shops and cafés afterwards.

Arminiushalle

Bremerstraße, 9 (map I, D1)
Mon.-Fri. 7.30am-6pm,
Sat. 7.30am-2pm
U-Bahn Turmstraße.

Classed as listed buildings, these covered markets are over a century old and are closely linked to the history of Moabit. The district was founded in 1716 by the Huguenots and named after the 'land of Moab' in the Bible. It was reputed to stand on infertile ground, but tradition has it that the French successfully grew asparagus here. The fact remains that throughout the 19th century the district grew up around business, the breweries and the fruit and vegetable trade. The covered markets are the

Marheinekehalle

Marheinekeplatz, 15
map III, D1)
Mon.-Fri. 7.30am-6pm,
Sat. 7.30am-2pm
U-Bahn Gneisenaustraße.

of a local market, wandering freely between the fruit and vegetable stalls, piled high with fresh produce, investigating the fish from the Baltic Sea or the local Brandenburg charcuterie at the delicatessen counters, this is a good place to come. For the sweet-toothed, the market is also the ideal place to satisfy your hankering for pastries or bread made from countless combinations of grains. If your outing gives you an appetite, you can sample some of the many specialities on offer on the stalls.

you'll plunge straight into the everyday life of the inhabitants of Kreuzberg here and even seem to travel back a little in time. Everything seems to hark back to the 1950s and 1960s, from the costermonger located next to the ladies' hairdresser, the tailor's shop adjacent to the butcher's. In the centre a square that rings with southern accents, the old 19th-century covered market has become a miniature town. Casual shoppers, young and alike, wander through the market throughout the day without a care in the world. Time seems to pass more slowly here, it's because you're in Kreuzberg, where time is a protected treasure.

last remaining vestiges of this era and as you make your way around them, you'll encounter a bazaar-like atmosphere that ties in with their slogan 'all under one roof'.

Born-Markt im Forum Steglitz

Schloßstraße, 1
(off map)
Mon.-Fri. 9am-7pm,
Sat. 9am-4pm
U-Bahn Walter-Schreiber-Platz.

If you get a sudden urge to soak up the atmosphere

BOOKS, RECORDS AND COMICS

Even if Berlin doesn't have a book fair like Frankfurt or Leipzig, the city of Brecht nevertheless has a multitude of small, specialist bookshops where it's a pleasure to linger. On the musical side, techno still rules, but is happy to share its throne with many other types of music. Diversity is everything here and the culture is hip hop.

Artificium

Rosenthaler Straße, 40-41 (map II, D1)
☎ 87 22 80
Mon. 1-9pm, Tue.-Thu. 10am-9pm, Fri. 10am-11pm, Sat. 10am-midnight, Sun. 11am-7pm
U-Bahn Hackescher Markt.

A strategic location in the Hackesche Höfe and opening hours worthy of the capitals of southern Europe help to make this book and card shop an ideal place for tourists seeking souvenirs of their visit to Berlin. Covering everything from sculpture and painting to architecture, you won't leave this living catalogue of the city's treasures empty-handed.

Bücherbogen

Kochstraße, 19 (map II, C2)
☎ 251 13 45
Mon.-Fri. 10am-8pm, Sat. 10am-4pm
U-Bahn Kochstraße.

A stone's throw from Checkpoint Charlie, this bookshop specialises in photography, design, architecture and town planning to keep fans of the avant-garde happy. Its modern architecture (1991) is supposed to be a free interpretation of the 1906 building housing the trendy Italian restaurant *Sale e Tabacchi*. The bookshop, in the

heart of the press district, is frequented by journalists from the alternative daily, *Tageszeitung*, whose offices are nearby.

Space Hall

Zossener Straße, 33 (map III, D1)
☎ 69 40 78 45
Mon.-Wed. 11am-7pm, Thu.-Fri. 11am-8pm, Sat. 10am-4pm
U-Bahn Gneisenaustraße.

In a street almost entirely devo to music of every kind, everyth that house, trance, soul and hi hop has to offer, in the way of frenetic rhythms and wild sequences, can be found here. The clientele are mainly stude and the bohemian spirit of the district makes it like a mini Woodstock – you could meet some really spaced-out custom here!

Kiepert

**Hardenbergstraße, 4-5
(map I, C2))
☎ 31 18 80
Mon.-Fri. 9am-8pm,
Sat. 9am-4pm
U-Bahn Ernst-Reuter-Platz.**

Every Berlin student is familiar
with this place. The family
bookshop near the technical
university and school of fine
art has spawned branches
throughout Berlin. But for
anyone in search of the most
up-to-date scientific work or the
latest must-read novel in either
English or German, the mother
store remains the first stop and
ultimate source.

WIENS LADEN & VERLAG

**Linienstraße, 158
(map II, C1)
☎ 28 38 53 52
Tue.-Fri. 2-7pm,
Sat. noon-5pm
U-Bahn Oranienburger
Straße.**

This place is a little treasure
chest with a character all its
own. It's a gallery, bookshop
and publishing house rolled
into one, stressing the affinity
between books and art. The
works on display here are
genuine limited editions
illustrated with original
lithographs or engravings.
If you fall under their spell,
you'll take away the memory
of knowing you've found
something exclusive.

Grober Unfug

**Zossener Straße, 32-33
(map III, D1)
☎ 69 40 14 92
Mon.-Fri. 11am-7pm,
Sat.11am-4pm
U-Bahn Gneisenaustraße.**

OK, so Belgium is the king of
continental comic books and
Germany isn't exactly renowned
for its sense of humour, yet
Berlin is certainly very creative
in the area of cartoon comics.
If you need convincing, come
along to this shop, where you'll
discover German graphics as
well as comic books from all
over the world, some of which
are rare collectors items. If you're
a fan of the original drawings,
you'll love the temporary
exhibitions – provided you
don't mind the German speech
bubbles.

Marga Schöller

**Knesebeckstraße, 33
(map I, C3)
☎ 881 11 12
Mon.-Wed. 9.30am-7pm,
Thu.-Fri. 9.30am-8pm,
Sat. 10am-4pm
U-Bahn Savignyplatz.**

Bookshops and
secondhand booksellers
have slowly but surely
infiltrated the area around
Savignyplatz. Marga Schöller's
has a quiet, muffled atmosphere
that's favourable to reading in
public. The accent is on the
literature of the English-speaking
world, with a predominance of
theatre, poetry and film scripts,
but there are plenty of children's
books as well.

Prinz Eisenherz

**Bleibtreustraße, 52
(map I, C3)
☎ 313 99 36
Mon.-Fri. 10am-7pm,
Sat. 10am-4pm
U-Bahn Savignyplatz.**

Always unconventional and
throwing conservatism to the
winds, Berlin has welcomed gay
cultural input with open arms.
In late June the city becomes
the scene of a wild carnival on
Christopher Street Day as the
main event of Gay Action Week.
It's therefore hardly surprising
that this bookshop, specialising
in gay literature, appears to
be one of the best-stocked in
the world.

Mr Dead & Mrs Free

**Bülowstraße, 5 (map III, B1)
☎ 215 14 49
Mon.-Wed. 11am-7pm,
Thu.-Fri. 11am-8pm,
Sat. 11am-4pm
U-Bahn Nollendorfplatz.**

This record shop is frequented
by Berlin's leading DJs, and is
easily the oldest and best in the
city. Connoisseurs had been
coming here for a long time
before it became an

institution.
Among the many
records on offer, expect
to find mainly imported
independent labels and turn your
attention to the Indie music
department, where you'll find
you're spoilt for choice.

Nightlife Practicalities

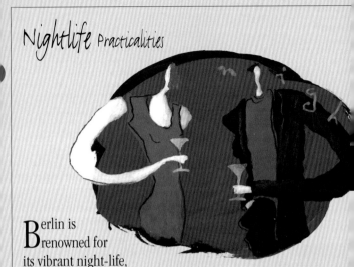

B erlin is renowned for its vibrant night-life, a tradition dating back to its heyday in the 1920s. Few cities offer such a dazzling range of night-time entertainment, from classical music concerts and alternative clubs to techno nightclubs and fringe theatres. The choice is vast and Berlin nights are long. You're sure to find what you're looking for.

won't have any difficulty getting into one of the city's many clubs. However, if you want to have a meal in a luxury restaurant or spend an evening at the opera, it's a good idea to pack something more dressy to wear. But here too, there are no precise rules and tolerance is the order of the day.

WHERE TO GO

After the fall of the Wall, Berliners deserted the Ku'damm, Kreuzberg and Schöneberg districts in favour of the new techno highspots of East Berlin, especially those in Mitte and Prenzlauer Berg. Cleaned-up and restored in next to no time, Mitte has become a chic, trendy district favoured by Berliners and tourists alike. In the more cosmopolitan Prenzlauer Berg, the alternative scene still rubs shoulders with residents of the old east and

a new trendy set of affluent people who congregate in the Kollwitzplatz. Despite this shift of Berliners to the east, Kreuzberg is still the centre of the alternative scene and Schöneberg the trendy, convivial haunt of students and the gay scene.

WHAT TO WEAR

Berliners attach little importance to clothes and generally dress quite casually. Whether you go in for a trendy, traditional, way-out or casual look, you normally

CLUBS AND BARS

As you'll soon have the chance to see for yourself, the night-owl is king in Berlin. A good number of bars, clubs and *Kneipen* wait for the last customers to leave before closing. This tolerant attitude, which is unique in Germany, is a form of compensation left over from the time of the Wall. It accounts for the intensity of Berlin nightlife, which can begin as early as 6 or 7 in the evening and only end late the following morning.

FINDING OUT WHAT'S ON

Berlin nightlife isn't only plentiful, it's also constantly changing. To avoid disappointment, it's always best to check the programme before you go. *Zitty* and *Tip* are the two essential magazines for finding out what's on. They have exhaustive listings of every kind of night-time entertainment, as well as the various cultural events taking place. Published fortnightly, they cost DM4.50 and 5 respectively.

The more glamorous review *Prinz* is aimed at a young, trendy audience, while the magazines *Flyer* and *030* concentrate on techno news and are distributed free in all the trendy shops, clubs and cafés in the city. *Sergej*, which is also free, is aimed at a gay audience. Flyers (see p. 23), widely distributed in record shops, clothes shops, clubs and cafés will be your best guide to the famous underground clubs.

Besides the reviews *Tip* and *Zitty*, you'll find a column or cultural supplement in the Berlin dailies, *Berliner Morgenpost*, *Berliner Zeitung*, *Tagesspiegel* and *Taz*, which will give you information about the dates and times of shows. The Berlin tourist information office publishes a twice-yearly bilingual magazine in German and English listing all the cultural events taking place in the city.

Lastly, for DM6, the brand-new magazine *Kultur pur* will give you very precise information about the plans of the various venues and the content of the many events, and is well worth the price.

BOOKING SEATS

As far as theatres, concerts and operas are concerned, it's possible to buy tickets on the evening of the performance, as box offices generally open an hour before the curtain goes up. However, you'll often need to arrive very early to get seats. If you want to see a successful play or grand opera, it's best to book several days in advance. In the case of the Philarmonia, it's even strongly advisable to book before you leave home.

You can book direct by phone, but you have to collect your tickets an hour before the start of the performance. The best plan is to go along to the concert hall or theatre or one of the city's many ticket offices. If you want to book seats before leaving home, the tourist information office is your best bet.

Berlin Tourism Marketing
☎ 25 00 25,
✆ 25 00 24 24.

Berlin Ticket
Potsdamerstr., 96
☎ 23 08 82 30,
✆ 23 08 82 99.

JAZZ CLUBS

Quasimodo

Kantstraße, 12a
(map I, C2-3)
☎ 312 80 86
From 5-9pm,
concerts from 9pm
U-Bahn Savignyplatz.

If you like jazz, blues and soul, this club, with its relaxed, intimate atmosphere, is the place for you. As well as staging high-quality concerts, the Quasimodo attracts international stars, especially during the jazz festival in the autumn (see p. 13).

A-Trane

Bleibtreustraße, 1
(map I, C3)
☎ 313 25 50
Every day,
concerts start at 10pm
U-Bahn Savignyplatz.

The A-Trane is the club for true jazz fans – even the most purist. In this intimate setting, you'll hear a wide range of jazz music, from be-bop to modern by way of free jazz.

b-flat

Rosenthaler Straße, 13
(map II, C-D1)
☎ 283 31 23
Entrance DM8,
concerts start at 10pm
U-Bahn Rosenthaler Platz.

In the four short years since it opened, this simple, sober club located in the trendy Mitte district has earned itself a considerable reputation. Performers here have included not only Berlin jazz groups but also top American acts.

BARS AND *KNEIPEN*

Green Door

Winterfeldtstraße, 50
(map I, D3)
☎ 215 25 15
From 6pm
U-Bahn Viktoria-Luise-Platz.

The Green Door has a well-earned reputation as one of the best bars in the city. Your cocktail is prepared as carefully as if it were the elixir of life. The highly original decor wavers between art, design and kitsch. The place is often packed and attracts the cool and trendy of Schöneberg.

Bar am Lützowplatz

Lützowplatz, 7
(map II, A3)
☎ 262 68 07

Every day, 5pm-4am,
happy hour 5-9pm
U-Bahn Nollendorfplatz.

Famous for enormous b (nearly 17m/5 long), the styli Bar am Lützo platz is a clas bar that regula attracts a ch well-heeled client of journalists a television profess nals. The cocktails on the expensive s but they're prepared by expe

Galerie Bremer

Fasanenstraße, 37
(map I, C3)
☎ 881 49 08
Mon.-Sat. from 8pm
U-Bahn Uhlandstraße.

This bar, in a room at the b of the famous Galerie Brem is a hidden treasure. Its dri are delicious, but what re makes it worth a visit are specially commissioned de and furniture designed by architect of the Berl Philharmonie, Hans Schar himself. Don't miss it. regular clientele is made u artists and others who lik come here to discuss ar simply to relax.

Reingold

Novalisstraße, 11
(map II, C1)
☎ 28 38 76 76
Tue.-Thu. 5pm-2am,
Fri.-Sat. 5pm-4am,
happy hour until 9pm
U-Bahn Oranienburger
Straße.

The Reingold is one of the very latest bars to have opened in the currently trendy Mitte district. To get in, you have to ring the bell of an impressive-looking metal door. Once inside, you'll find an elegant bar fitted out in 1920s-style. You can order oysters (*Austern*) to go with your drink.

The Pip's

Augustraße, 84
(map II, C1)
☎ 282 45 12
Sun.-Thu. 8pm-3am,
Fri.-Sat. 9pm-4am
U-Bahn Oranienburger
Straße.

The resolutely 1970s design of this bar, with its rounded forms and bright colours, attracts a young, cosmopolitan crowd, who come to drink cocktails and, later in the evening, to dance on the tiny dance floor to the sound of old disco, soul and funk.

Café M

Goltzstraße, 33
(map III, B1)
☎ 216 70 92
Mon.-Fri. 8-2am,
Sat.-Sun. 9-2am
U-Bahn
Nollendorfplatz.

One of the few trendy bars of the 1980s that has managed to retain its popularity into the 21st century. While the decor remains the same, the clientele has moved with the times. It's location at the heart of the Schöneberg 'scene' makes it a great place to start the evening.

Ankerklause

Maybachufer, on Kottbusser
Bridge (off map)
☎ 693 56 49
From 10am, Mon. 4pm
U-Bahn
Schönleinstraße.

This bar, which overlooks the Landwehrkanal, is one of the most pleasant in the district. In summer, you can watch the boats from the terrace and listen to alternative rock on the juke-box. On Thursdays, the bar becomes a club, with easy listening and drum'n'bass.

Würgeengel

Dresdnerstraße, 121
(map II, D2-3)
☎ 615 64 73
Every day, from 6pm,
food served until
midnight
U-Bahn
Moritzplatz.

With its magnificent period ceiling, crystal chandelier and crimson decor, this bar is one of the nicest in Kreuzberg. It has a relaxed atmosphere and friendly service, and is much frequented by the 'scene'.

CLUBS AND NIGHTCLUBS

WMF

**Johannisstraße, 20–21
(map II, C1)
Fri.–Sun. from 11pm
U-Bahn Oranienburger Straße.**

The WMF was one of Berlin's first big techno clubs. After a few moves, it has settled for the time being in a former residence for senior officials of the GDR. While the crowd are not all that awe-inspiring, the music and DJs are mostly excellent.

90 Grad

**Dennewitzstraße, 37
(map II, D3)
☎ 262 89 84
U-Bahn Bülowstraße.**

Before Berlin nightlife shifted to the East, the 90 Grad was one of the trendiest nightclubs in the West. In spite of the emigration, it's still one of the city's in-places, attracting a chic, relatively affluent crowd of regulars. Thursday is gay and drag queen night.

Kalkscheune

**Johannisstraße, 2
(map II, C1)
☎ 28 39 00 65
U-Bahn Oranienburger Straße.**

In a listed building a stone's throw from the WMF, the Kalkscheune offers a wide variety of club nights. With techno parties, tango nights, gay evenings, jazz concerts and variety shows, there's

something to suit all tastes. It's a good idea to consult listings magazines *Zitty* or *Tip* before you go.

Roter Salon

**Left wing of the Volksbühne,
Rosa-Luxemburg-Platz
(map II, D1)
☎ 28 59 89 38
U-Bahn Rosa-Luxemburg-Platz.**

With its large chandeliers and velvet armchairs, this wonderful retro lounge in the Volksbühne theatre is a fabulous place to dance the tango (on

Wednesdays) or salsa (on Tuesdays). Beginners are welcome at these fun evenings. On Mondays, drum 'n' bass takes over. See *Tip* or *Zitty* for the weekly programme.

Icon

**Cantianstraße, 15
(off map)
Thu.–Sun. from 11pm
U-Bahn Eberswalder Straße.**

Tucked away in the basement of a magnificent vaulted cellar this club is the home o drum'n'bass in Berlin. The rising stars from London and

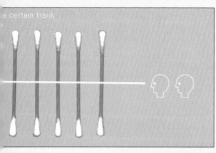

e certain frank

ristol come here to mix their
ounds. Big beat, hip hop,
eggae and house also feature
n the programme.

Kumpelnest 3000

itzowstraße, 23
(map II, A3)
☎ 261 69 18
every day from 5pm
-Bahn Nollendorfplatz.

his former brothel not far
om Potsdamer Platz was the
ecca of the Berlin scene in
e 1980s. With its original,
credibly kitsch decor, it's still
e choice for night-owls of all
,es and persuasions. A
ique place that's always full
bursting at the weekend.

Kat Club

ogauer Straße, 2
ff map)
611 38 33
ed.-Sun. from 11pm
Bahn Hermannplatz.

e of Berlin's hottest clubs,
h 'naked parties' (for men),
ather and latex' and 'Sex
ince Bizarre' evenings. You
n't get in unless you observe
dress code. Only for the un-
ibited and those in the know.

aria am
stbahnhof

aße der Pariser
mmune, 8-10
f map)

Wed.-Sun.
U-Bahn Weberwieser.

This former GDR post office
is where they're currently
playing the most experimental
electronic music, with concerts, DJ evenings and visual
installations. Even if it closes,
the Maria will have contribu-
ted to bringing the 'scene' to
this industrial corner of the
former East Berlin.

Schmalzwald BHG

Schlegelstraße, 26
(map II, C1)
Fri.-Sat.
U-Bahn Zinnowitzer Straße.

Tucked away in a rear courtyard, this club, with its amaz-

ing decor, is already something of a legend in Berlin.
The famous karaoke nights of
Gordon M. & Gordon W. probably have something to do
with it. The club has already
moved four times, so it's a
good idea to consult *Zitty*, *Tip*
or *Flyer* before going.

Tresor/Globus

Leipziger Straße, 126a
(map II, B2)
Wed.-Sun. from 11pm
U-Bahn Potsdamer Platz.

One of the oldest techno clubs
in Berlin, where DJs from the
early days, such as Motte, Rock
and Tanith, perform. A legend.

Matrix

Warschauer Platz, 18
(off map)
☎ 29 49 10 47
Fri.-Sat. from 10pm
U-Bahn Warschauer Platz.

The best-known DJs in Berlin
(Westbam, Marusha, Hous-
meister, etc.) regularly come
to mix in this vast, hangar-like
space. For weekday evenings,
watch the flyers.

CONCERTS, OPERAS AND THEATRES

Berliner Philarmonie

Matthäikirchstraße, 1
(map II, B2)
☎ 25 48 81 32
Bookings Mon.-Fri. noon-6pm, Sat.-Sun. and holidays 11am-2pm
U-Bahn Potsdamer Platz.

Words cannot describe Hans Scharoun's masterpiece,which opened in 1963. The arrival in 1989 of Claudio Abbado, the successor to Herbert von Karajan, marked a change of direction, with a programme more strongly orientated towards contemporary works.

Deutsche Staatsoper

Unter den Linden, 5-7
(map II, C2)
☎ 20 35 45 55
Box office Mon.-Fri. 10am-6pm, Sat.-Sun. and hols 2-6pm. Tel. bookings Mon.-Sat. 10am-8pm, Sun. 10am-6pm
U-Bahn Französische Straße.

Founded in 1742 at the behest of Friedrich II, the Staatsoper is the oldest opera house in Berlin and by far the most beautiful. Since his arrival in 1992, conductor Daniel Barenboim seems to have restored the opera to some of its former glory, with a repertoire of high-quality operas, ballets and concerts.

Deutsche Oper

Bismarckstraße, 35
(map I, B2)
☎ 343 84 01
Bookings Mon.-Sat. 11am, Sun. 10am-2pm, until 1 hr before the performance
U-Bahn Deutsche Oper.

Built in 1961, this West Berlin opera house was intended to make up for the loss of the other big opera houses in the east of the city. Since then, the Deutsche Oper has won international acclaim thanks to great conductors, stars from all over the world and excellent acoustics. Götz Friedrich's productions of Wagner's Ring Cycle are among the best.

Schaubühne am Lehniner Platz

Kurfürstendamm, 153
(map I, B3)
☎ 89 00 23
Box office Mon.-Sat. 11am-6.30pm, Sun and holidays from 3pm
U-Bahn Adenauerplatz.

For a long time, this We Berlin theatre owed its repu tation to the work of directo Peter Stein and producer Lu Bondy. The recent arrival of a unconventional young dire tor, Thomas Ostmeier, cou give the Schaubühne a ne lease of life.

Berliner Ensembl

Bertolt-Brecht-Platz, 1
(map II, C1)
☎ 282 31 60
Bookings Mon.-Sat. 11am-6pm, Sun. 3-6pm
U-Bahn Friedrichstraße.

Founded by Brecht in 194 the Berliner Ensemble the best possible showcase f his works. Since the death 1995 of its stage manager, t writer Heiner Müller, the has undergone a number changes of direction, sadly n always for the better. T appointment in Novemb 1999 of Claus Peymann, fo mer manager of the famo Vienna Burgtheater, was h led as a major event.

Volksbühne

Rosa-Luxemburg-Platz
(map II, D1)
☎ 247 67 72
Bookings daily, noon-6pm
U-Bahn Rosa-Luxemburg-
Platz.

After the fall of the Wall, the
Volksbühne became the scene
of a form of experimental
theatre masterminded by its
East German manager Frank
Castorf. It has been accused of
running out of steam recently,
but is still one of the most
interesting and innovative
theatres in Berlin.

Theater des Westens

Kantstraße, 12
(map I, C2-3)
☎ 882 28 88
Box office Tue.-Sat. noon-
6pm, Sun. 2-5pm. Tel.
Bookings Mon.-Fri. 10am-
6pm, Sat. 10am-4pm
U-Bahn Zoologischer Garten.

Under the leadership of its
manager and director Helmut
Baumann, this sumptuous
theatre has in just a few years
become one of the leading
musical comedy venues in
Europe. Besides smash hits
such as *Cabaret* and *La Cage
aux Folles*, the theatre also
stages classic musicals and
original works from around
the world.

Bar Jeder Vernunft

Schaperstraße, 24
(map I, C3)
☎ 883 15 82
Tickets sold Mon.-Sun.
noon-8.30pm
U-Bahn Spichernstraße.

The Art Nouveau-style tent
lined with red velvet and covered in mirrors is part of the
attraction here. In addition to
the magical atmosphere,
you'll enjoy songs and cabaret
performed with great charis-
ma by the artists, who are
either already well-known or
are on the way to being so.

Chamäleon Varieté

Rosenthaler Straße, 40/41
(map II, D1)
☎ 282 71 18
Mon.-Thu. noon-9pm,
Fri.-Sat. noon-mid., Sun
4-9pm
U-Bahn Weinmeisterstraße.

The Chamäleon, housed in
one of the Art Nouveau rooms
of the Hackeschen Höfen, is the
most original of avant-garde
variety theatres. The diverse
performances are by turns gra-
ting, hilarious, off the wall and
poetical. On Fridays and
Saturdays, the midnight
shows, with their last-minute
guests, are always good for a
memorable evening.

Sophiensaele

Sophienstraße, 18
(map II, C1)
☎ 283 52 66
Box office opens 1 hour
before the performance
U-Bahn Weinmeisterstraße.

Currently the in-place for free
theatre in Berlin. Where Karl
Liebknecht once led the call for
revolution, talented and original young artists now deliver a
mixture of theatre, dance and
performance. Don't miss it.

Theater am Ufer

Tempelhofer Ufer, 10
(map II, B3)
☎ 251 31 16
U-Bahn Möckernbrücke.

Directed by the painter and
producer Andrej Woron, the
Theater Kreatur is an unconventional and avant-garde
troupe presenting visionary
visual shows. Unusual masks
and strange machines appear
out of nowhere to create a
Kafkaesque universe that's
worth a visit.

Conversion tables for clothes shopping

Women's sizes

Shirts/dresses

U.K	U.S.A	EUROPE
8	6	36
10	8	38
12	10	40
14	12	42
16	14	44
18	16	46

Sweaters

U.K	U.S.A	EUROPE
8	6	44
10	8	46
12	10	48
14	12	50
16	14	52

Shoes

U.K	U.S.A	EUROPE
3	5	36
4	6	37
5	7	38
6	8	39
7	9	40
8	10	41

Men's sizes

Shirts

U.K	U.S.A	EUROPE
14	14	36
$14^{1}/_{2}$	$14^{1}/_{2}$	37
15	15	38
$15^{1}/_{2}$	$15^{1}/_{2}$	39
16	16	41
$16^{1}/_{2}$	$16^{1}/_{2}$	42
17	17	43
$17^{1}/_{2}$	$17^{1}/_{2}$	44
18	18	46

Suits

U.K	U.S.A	EUROPE
36	36	46
38	38	48
40	40	50
42	42	52
44	44	54
46	46	56

Shoes

U.K	U.S.A	EUROPE
6	8	39
7	9	40
8	10	41
9	10.5	42
10	11	43
11	12	44
12	13	45

More useful conversions

1 centimetre	0.39 inches	1 inch	2.54 centimetres
1 metre	1.09 yards	1 yard	0.91 metres
1 kilometre	0.62 miles	1 mile	1. 61 kilometres
1 litre	1.76 pints	1 pint	0.57 litres
1 gram	0.35 ounces	1 ounce	28.35 grams
1 kilogram	2.2 pounds	1 pound	0.45 kilograms

This guide was written by **Véronique Souben** and **Alexandre Mazurek**, who would like to thank **Dorothée Köhler**, **Anita Gandon**, **Stéphane Bauer**, **Diane Josse**, **Albino Cipriano**, **Thomas Beier**, **Diane** and **Sébastien Landé** and all the staff of Stübli Delicatessen.

Series editor **Liz Coghill**
Translated by **Margaret Rocques**
Project manager and copy editor **Margaret Rocques**
Additional research and assistance **Sofi Mogensen**, **Jenny Piening**, **Maggie Ramsay**, **Christine Bell**, **Caroline Boissy** and **Aurélie Joiris**.

We have done our best to ensure the accuracy of the information contained in this guide. However, addresses, phone numbers, opening times etc inevitably do change from time to time, so if you find a discrepancy please do let us know. You can contact us at: hachetteuk@orionbooks.co.uk or write to us at Hachette UK, address below.

Hachette UK guides provide independent advice. The authors and compilers do not accept any remuneration for the inclusion of any addresses in these guides.

Please note that we cannot accept any responsibility for any loss, injury or inconvenience sustained by anyone as a result of any information or advice contained in this guide.

Photo acknowledgements

Inside pages
All photographs were taken by **Éric Guillot**, with the exception of the following:

Serge Attal, Ask Images: p. 3 (b.r.), p. 26 (t.r.), p. 32 (c.l. and b.r.), p. 33 (b.r.), p. 35; Patrick Lagery, Ask Images : p. 34 (c.c.), p. 50 (b.c.)
Gil Giuglio, Hémisphères: p. 38; **Maurizio Borgese, Hémisphères**: p. 39 (t.c.)
Photothèque Hachette: p. 12 (c.l.), p. 14 (b.l.), p. 15 (t.r. and b.l.) © Films sans Frontières, p. 16 (c.c.), p. 18 (b.l. and b.r.), p. 48 (b.c.)
Nicolas Edwige: p. 23 (c.l.), p. 42 (b.r.), p. 55 (t.c.), p. 65 (b.l. and c.r.), p. 75 (b.l.), p. 76 (c.c.)
Jacques Debru: p. 24 (t.r. and c.r.), p. 25 (c.r.), p. 46 (b.)
Philippe Fournier: p. 26 (b.r.)

Illustrations: **Monique Prudent**

First published in the United Kingdom in 2000 by Hachette UK

Distributed in the United States by Sterling Publishing Co., Inc.
387 Park Avenue South, New York, NY 10016-8810

A CIP catalogue for this book is available from the British Library

ISBN 1 84202 061 7

Hachette UK, Cassell & Co., The Orion Publishing Group, Wellington House, 125 Strand, London WC2R 0BB

Printed and bound in Italy by Milanostampa S.P.A.

If you're staying on a little longer and would like to try some new places, the following pages will provide you with a wide choice of hotels, restaurants and bars, listed by district. Though you can just turn up at the door of a restaurant and have a meal (except in the most prestigious establishments), don't forget to book your hotel several days in advance (see p. 70).
Prices are a guide only.
Enjoy your stay!

STAYING ON A LITTLE LONGER

If you're staying on a little longer, you'll find below a varied selection of establishments ranging from modest but high-quality pensions to luxury hotels. Most have been chosen for their original character and central location. For those who like peace, quiet and greenery, we've included a few less central addresses. The prices given are for double rooms.

Prenzlauer Berg

Hotel Jurine
Schwedter Straße, 15
☎ 44 32 99-0
🖷 44 32 99 99
Around DM190.
One of the few hotels with all mod cons in Penzlauer Berg. Its light, airy rooms and location in the heart of the district make it a very pleasant place to stay. From here, it only takes a few minutes to reach the many bars and cafés in the neighbourhood of Kollwitzplatz .

Hotel Kastanienhof
Kastanienallee, 65
☎ 44 30 50
🖷 44 30 51 11
DM160-265.
This small local hotel in the heart of the trendy alternative scene of Prenzlauer Berg, has the old-fashioned but cosy charm of East German homes. If you want a glimpse of Berlin before the fall of the Wall, this is an ideal place to stay.

Hotel Gustavo-Sorat
Prenzlauer Allee, 169
☎ 446 61-0
🖷 446 61-661
Around DM260.
An original hotel, amusingly decorated in a bright, colourful way by the Spanish painter, Gustavo. Although it isn't very close to the centre, Prenzlauer Allee is the main Prenzlauer Berg road leading directly to Alexanderplatz and the television tower.

Hakescherhof (Mitte)

Hotel Taunus
Monbijouplatz, 1
☎ 283 52 54
🖷 283 52 55
Around. DM180.
A simple but pleasant hotel run by a friendly team of staff with two main advantages: it benefits from the peace and quiet of Monbijou Park, yet is only a stone's throw from the trendy nightlife of Mitte.

Friedrichstrasse (Mitte)

Hotel Maritim Pro Arte
Friedrichstraße, 151
☎ 2033-5
🖷 20 33 42 09
Around DM370.
The Maritim is one of the very first luxury hotels to have appeared in this strategic part of Mitte shortly after the fall of the Wall. Resolutely post-89, the chain called on great names of design, such as Philippe Stark and well-known German neo-Expressionist painters (Salomé, Fetting, etc.) to decorate the vast lobby and other areas. A luxury hotel with a swimming pool and the largest conference room in Mitte.

Unter den Linden★★
Unter den Linden, 14
☎ 23 81 10
🖷 23 81 11 00
Around DM160.
If you're curious to know what a luxury hotel was like under the former GDR, the Unter den Linden is the place to come. Very little seems to have changed here, not even the cosmopolitan clientele. The rooms may be small, but the hotel's unique location on the corner of Friedrichstraße and Unter den Linden more than makes up for the inconvenience. The 1970s breakfast room is worth a visit in itself.

Alexanderplatz (Mitte)

Forum Hotel Berlin★★★★
Alexanderplatz
☎ 23 89-0
🖷 23 89-43 05

E-mail: forumberlin@inter-conti.com
Around DM280.
A hotel unique for its size (it resembles a skyscraper), number of rooms (1,006) and excellent location in Alexanderplatz (opposite the television tower). Recently refurbished with all mod cons, this almost legendary GDR establishment offers an uninterrupted view of the heart of the former East Berlin. Highly recommended to fans of Alexanderplatz and those with a fascination for the former GDR.

Anhalter Bahnhof

Hotel Stuttgarterhof
Anhalter Straße, 9
☎ 264 83-0
🖷 264 83-900
E-mail: 0302264830@t-online.de
Around DM280.
A comfortable hotel much sought-after for its central location between Potsdamer Platz and Friedrichstraße. The relatively spacious rooms have a warm, rustic decor with furnishings of dark wood. In the inner courtyard, the large red-brick façade with wide lattice windows is in a typical Berlin style.

Kurfürstendamm (Charlottenburg)

Steinberger★★★★★
Los-Angeles-Platz
☎ 21 27-0
🖷 212 71 17
Around DM400, breakfast DM31.
The Steinberger is a much-sought-after luxury hotel in Charlottenburg. Businessmen and well-known personalities from the film and pop worlds stay here. The hotel owes its success to its warm decor, first-class service and excelle... location in a quiet square – all just a few minutes from the Ku'damm.

Savoy★★★★
Fasanenstraße, 9-10
☎ 311 03 0
🖷 311 03 333
E-mail: info@hotel-savoy.com

Around DM320,
breakfast DM28.
*With its large chandeliers,
leather armchairs and red
curtains, this luxury hotel is
sure to remind you of the
set of an old black and white
movie. In fact, for over seventy
years, a large number of
writers, composers, actors,
scientists and poets have
passed through its doors and
become part of its history.
A British-style bar completes
the picture.*

Hotel-Pension
Fasanhaus
Fasanenstraße/
Ku'damm
☎ 881 67 13
🅵 882 39 47
Around DM110
(no credit cards).
*A family pension pleasantly
furnished in the spirit of
1900 in one of the finest
streets in Charlottenburg.
In spite of its setting in the
immediate vicinity of the
Ku'damm, it's a quiet place
with a warm, friendly welcome.
The entrance hall has superb
Art Nouveau decoration.*

Sorat Art'otel
Joachimsthaler Straße, 29
☎ 884 47-0
🅵 884 47-700
E-mail: art-otel@sorat-
hotels.com
Around DM260.
*One of the former members
of the Fluxus group, Wolf
Vostell, was given a free
hand in designing this hotel
belonging to the Sorat group,
just a stone's throw from
the Ku'damm. Furniture with
bold lines and unusual, modern
pictures have turned it into
an art and design gallery.
Fans of contemporary art will
be delighted.*

Kempinski Hotel
Bristol★★★★★
Kurfürstendamm, 27
☎ 884 34-0
🅵 883 60 75
Around DM500.
*Once the 1950s, the recently
renamed Kempinski has been
a privileged establishment
frequented by Berlin high
society and VIPs. A swimming*

pool, sauna, fitness centre
and chauffeur-driven limousines
are naturally part of the service.
The hotel also has a gourmet
restaurant whose setting on
the corner of the Ku'damm
makes it the ideal place to see
and be seen.*

Askanischer Hof
Kurfürstendamm, 53
☎ 881 80 33
🅵 881 72 06
Around DM250.
*A Ku'damm hotel with all
the charm of yesteryear. The
breakfast room, furnished with
magnificent furniture dating
from the time of the Kaiser,
sets the tone. The hotel's
old-fashioned atmosphere
is probably what has attracted
the stars of stage and screen
to it for years during the Berlin
Film Festival.*

**Savignyplatz
(Charlottenburg)**

Art-Nouveau
Hotel-pension
Leibnizstraße, 59
☎ 327 744 0
🅵 327 744 40
E-mail: hotelartnou-
veau@snfu.de
Around DM240.
*This brand-new hotel on the
4th floor of an old building
is a place to remember. Art
Deco furniture and modern
design sit side-by-side in
extremely elegant, personalised
rooms. As yet little-known,
the hotel is sure to please
the more discerning client.
Don't miss the lovely period
lift, with its small seats, in
the lobby.*

Pension Kettler
Bleibtreustraße, 19
☎ 883 49 49
🅵 883 56 76
Around DM165
(no credit cards).
*A pension full of style and
character run by a keen
collector of art and antiques.
There are works of art in the
corridors, and the rooms,
superbly furnished in different
styles, such as the 1900s,
English, Toulouse Lautrec or
Napoleonic, are all little gems.
It's a place whose reputation is
passed on by word of mouth.*

HOTELS

Adenauer Platz (Charlottenburg)

Hotel Charlottenburger Hof
Stuttgarter Platz, 14
☎ 32 90 70
📠 32 33 723
E-mail:
charlottenburger.hof@t-online.de
Around DM180,
breakfast DM9.
A hotel with a colourful decor inspired by Miró, Kandinsky, Picasso, Dali and Mondrian. There are posters by the artists on every floor and the rooms are individually and originally decorated. Good value for money.

Wilmersdorf

Frauenhotel Artemisia
Brandenburgischestraße, 18
☎ 873 89 05
📠 862 86 53
E-mail: Frauenhotel-Berlin@t-online.de
Around DM198.
The Artemisia, which is on the 4th and 5th floors of an early 20th-century building, was the first hotel in Germany designed exclusively for women. No men are allowed here, and it's very popular. Since its opening in 1989, this tastefully decorated hotel has been a great success. In summer, the roof terrace, with a view across Berlin is a popular place for a generous, elegant breakfast.

Pension München
Güntzelstraße, 62
☎ 85 79 12-0
📠 85 79 12-22
Around DM100,
breakfast DM9.
You'll get a very friendly welcome at this pension which is run by a sculptress. Apart from the prettily-decorated rooms, you're sure to fall for the charming breakfast room with its white lilies.

Schöneberg

Arco Hotel★★
Geisbergstraße, 30
☎ 235 148-0
📠 211 33 87
Around DM140.
A very pleasant little hotel and one of the few in the quiet, affluent district of Schöneberg. From here you can reach the bars and cafés of the district in just a few minutes and you'll be only a stone's throw from the charming Viktoria-Luise-Platz. The rooms come in a wide variety of sizes and those with a small sitting-room are highly recommended.

Kreuzberg

Gasthaus Dietrich Herz
Marheinekeplatz, 15
☎/📠 693 11 73
From DM120
(no credit cards).
A picturesque hotel-inn inside the oldest covered market in Berlin. The rooms are simple but they open onto one of the most charming squares in Berlin, offering a fascinating view of the life of the Kiez district.

Tiergarten

Sorat Hotel Spree Bogen★★★
Alt-Moabit, 99
☎ 399 20-0
📠 399 20-999
E-mail: spree-bogen@SORAT-Hotels.com
Around DM350.
Another hotel belonging to the Sorat group located, this time, in a former waterside dairy. An ultra-modern establishment combining industrial charm, up-to-the-minute architecture and contemporary design. If, in spite of its originality, it seems a little too far from the centre, it's worth bearing in mind that the U- and S-Bahn stations are only 2 or 3 minutes away. But the riverboat or hotel yacht are really a must and will take you to the city centre in a trice.

Charlottenburg Castle

Schloßpakhotel
Heubnerweg, 2a
☎ 326 90 30
📠 325 88 61
Around DM225.
A comfortable, traditional hotel with a privileged setting on the edge of Charlottenburg Palace park. Most of the rooms, as you would imagine, have a view of the park. A marvellous place for a relaxing walk after a day's shopping.

Hotel Seehof am Lietzensee
Lietzenseeufer, 11
☎ 320 02 0
📠 320 02 251
E-mail: HOTEL_SEEHOF _BERLIN@t-online.de
Around DM280,
breakfast DM25.
Though a little far from the centre, this hotel has an ideal setting on the banks of a lake beside a park. It's probably this setting that attracts singers to the Seehof in summer, when they come to Berlin to perform on the stage of the Waldbühne. The magnificent terrace overhanging the lake and surrounded by greenery is an ideal place for a cocktail or dinner for two.

Grunewald

Hotel-Pension Alpina
Trabener Straße, 3
☎ 891 35 17
or 991 60 90
📠 893 53 42
Around DM140.
If you who want to get away from the hustle and bustle of the city, this family-run pension in an elegant early 20th-century villa is an ideal place to stay. As well as being located in a quiet Grunewald street, the hotel will delight you with its old-fashioned charm and plush furnishings in the style of the period.

HOTELS

GOURMET CUISINE

Bamberger Reiter
Regensburger Straße, 7
Schöneberg
☎ 218 42 82
Tue.-Sat. 6-10pm.
This Schöneberg restaurant has for years been one of the leading gourmet establishments in the city. In a noble rustic decor, you'll be served carefully-prepared regional dishes, such as chanterelle mushroom tartare with asparagus salad (around DM145 for a 6-course set meal). For more modest budgets, the restaurant has a bistrot, the Ranerburgers, where you can enjoy less sophisticated but equally outstanding cuisine.

First Flour
(in the Palace Hotel),
Budapester Straße, 38
Charlotttenburg
☎ 25 02 10 20
Mon.-Fri. noon-2.30pm,
6-11.30pm,
Sat. 6-11.30pm.
This luxury restaurant on the first floor of the large Palace Hotel is one of the most highly-rated restaurants in Berlin. It owes its renown to its chef, Rolf Schmidt, whose meticulously thought-out dishes have earned him a star (set meals from DM145). Apart from its high-quality cuisine, the restaurant possesses one of the biggest French wine cellars in the city.

Grand Slam
Gottfried-von-Gramm-Weg, 47-45
Dahlem
☎ 825 38 19
Tue.-Sat. 6.30-11pm.
Tennis fans are familiar with this hotel a stone's throw from Steffi Graff's famous training club. Apart from its setting, this restaurant, with the air of an English manor house, is renowned for the culinary creations of its chef, Johannes King. The duck with chanterelle mushrooms is just one example among many.

Ana e Bruno
Sophie-Charlotten-Str., 101
☎ 325 71 10

Every day except Sun.-Mon. 6pm-midnight.
It's undoubtedly because of the creative talents of its chef, Bruno Pellegrini, that this Italian restaurant is often named the best in the city. He's known for his successful culinary experiments, especially when it comes to reinterpreting the old recipes of his region. There's a wide choice of mainly Italian wines.

Kaiserstuben
Am Kupfergraben, 6a
Mitte
☎ 20 45 29 80
Tue.-Sat. 6pm-1am.
This restaurant is opposite the Pergamommuseum and located a few metres/yards below street level. It's small in size but big on quality and the dishes, which are aristocratically cuisined by its rising young star, Tim Raue, have recently earned it a star (1998). It's the ideal place for a gourmet end to a visit to the museum of ancient art.

SMART AND ELEGANT

Lubitsch
Bleibtreu Straße, 47
Charlottenburg
☎ 882 37 56
Mon.-Sat. 9am-midnight,
Sun. from 6pm.
A quietly elegant bistrot in the neighbourhood of Savignyplatz which serves simple but high-quality bistrot-type specialities, such as poached fillet of beef with mustard or the more basic 'Lubitsch Burger'. Discreet, pleasant service and, in summer, a terrace which is ideally located to observe the life of the district.

Maxwell
Bergstr., 22
Mitte
☎ 280 71 21
Every day 6pm-midnight,
in summer noon-midnight.
This restaurant on the northern-most edge of Mitte is unquestionably the smartest in the district. You'll definitely be charmed by the elegant rear courtyard and former

brasserie with its neo-Gothic architecture in which the Maxwell has taken up residence. The high-quality, refined cuisine is equal to the setting, as are the wines.

Paris-Moskau
Alt-Moabit, 141
Tiergarten
☎ 394 20 81
Every day 6pm-1am.
Who would have thought that this old building situated on the former Paris-Moscow railway line and surrounded by building sites hides one of Berlin's most popular smart restaurants? It's a charming setting for light, innovative cuisine based on regional products. The duck's liver terrine with pickled red onions and the black radish mousse with smoked eels are worth a visit in themselves.

Emelerhaus
Märkisches Ufer, 10
Mitte
☎ 24 06 29 04
Tue.-Sat. 6-10.30pm,
Sun. noon-3pm.
In the 1970s and 1980s, the Emerlerhaus was already the most renowned gourmet restaurant in the GDR. Now associated to the ultramodern Art'otel, (see p. 3 of the coloured pages), it has never-theless retained the character of an old patrician house, with a superb mid-18th century Rococo decor. A very high-class setting for light, elegant seasonal cuisine.

Lutter & Wegner
Charlottenstr., 56
☎ 20 29 54 10
Every day 11am-11pm.
A legendary restaurant founded in 1811 in the magnificent Gendarmenmarkt square and later destroyed in the war. Since its recent re-opening in 1997, Lutter & Wegner has quickly become known for its home cooking and high-class wines. A boutique and wine merchant's still form part of the establishment. Since the 1950s, it has had an equally smart and elegant offshoot located in Charlottenburg, Schlüterstaße 55.

EXOTIC

Fukagawa
Pfalzburger Straße, 20,
Wilmersdorf
☎ 873 72 95.
*This restaurant with a very
minimalist Japanese decor
serves genuine Japanese
cuisine prepared the traditional
way. The Teppanyaki dishes
are highly recommended.
Pieces of fish (as well as meat),
vegetables and mushrooms
are thrown directly onto a large
hotplate and cooked before
your very eyes by expert hands.
Quite delicious.*

Brazil
Gormannstraße, 22
Mitte
☎ 28 59 90 26
Every day 6pm-2am.
*More than just a Brazilian
restaurant appreciated for its
cuisine and service, the Brazil
is first and foremost a Kneipe
much frequented by the 'scene'.
Go for the starters in a variety
of flavours, including pancakes
filled with vegetables or cod
(DM15). In summer, the shady
inner courtyard is the ideal
place to enjoy a well-mixed
Caïpirinhas (the summer cocktail that's a must in Berlin).*

Hitit
Knobelsdorffstraße, 35
Charlottenburg
☎ 322 45 57
Every day noon-midnight.
*The refined, fresh decor of
this restaurant is inspired by
the culture of the Hittites, the
ancient people of Anatolia
(20th-12th century BC). The
distinctive decor aside, the
Hitit is first and foremost one
of the very few restaurants
in Berlin to offer carefully-
prepared, inventive Turkish
cuisine. The terrace is pleasant
in summer.*

Kopenhagen
Kurfürstendamm, 203-205
☎ 881 62 19
Every day noon-1am.
*In the nice, cosy atmosphere
of a Danish sitting-room with
velvet armchairs, curtains,
tapestries and wall plates, you
can enjoy a wide choice of
Danish dishes and any amount*
of fish-based starters. You really
should try the specialities of
the week, which vary according
to the time of year and seasonal
produce.

TRADITIONAL

Raabe Diele
Emerlerhaus, Märkisches
Ufer, 107
Mitte
☎ 24 06 20.
*The cellars of the noble
Emelerhaus are home to a
Berlin tavern, the Raabe Diele.
Its decor is no less chic for
being rustic, with leather seats
and a smoking lounge. You'll
find all the great classics of
Berlin cuisine here, from
Eisbein (knuckle of pork) to
the house speciality, the Raabe
fry-up (Raabe-Pfanne). In
summer, you can also take
advantage of the terrace-
barge moored in front of the
restaurant.*

Henne
Leuschnerdamm, 25
Kreuzberg
☎ 614 77 30
Open Wed.-Sun. from
7pm.
*This charming establishment
with its rustic setting will give
you a good idea of the
atmosphere of late 19th-century
working-class Berlin. Only
one dish, the house speciality,
is served here: half a grilled
chicken (Milchmasthähnchen).
To accompany this dish, order
a portion of cabbage or potato
salad, unless of course, you'd
be satisfied with one of the
alcoholic specialities of the
house.*

Hardtke
Meinekestraße, 27a/b
☎ 881 98 27
Every day 11-1am.
*In this lively, rustic setting
in the neighbourhood of
the Ku'damm, you'll find
genuine Berlin cuisine, with
tasty dishes served in generous
portions. One of the house
specialities, 'Schlachteplatte
mit Molle und Korn', is a plate
of charcuterie, served with
beer and brandy to wash it all
down.*

TRENDY OR ORIGINAL

Je Länger Je Lieber
Göhrener Straße
Penzlauer Berg
☎ 441 22 95
Tue.-Sun. 6pm-2am.
This restaurant run by a former circus troupe, which is well decorated with GDR furniture and Art Deco objects, promises you memorable Friday and Saturday nights. The wild antics of the cooks/waiters/actors will make your meal an unforgettable experience.

Schell
Knesebeckstraße, 22
☎ 312 83 10
Every day 9am-midnight.
The Schell is one of the new, chic Italian restaurants with simple decor and minimalist dishes. Much prized by a trendy, affluent clientele, this bar-restaurant is the place of the moment, where you come to see and be seen more than to sample the Italian specialities. A Charlottenburg in-place that's not to be missed.

Schwarzenraben
Nneue Schönhauser
Straße, 13
☎ 28 39 16 98
Every day 10am-midnight.
In spite of its dark, austere decor, the Schwarzenraben is currently one of the most prominent places in Mitte. Film stars are even said to come here during the Berlin Film Festival. Here, too, the Italian cuisine is a secondary consideration, the main thing is to be here at the right time. There's a very chic bar with nice, comfortable leather arm-chairs in the basement.

Oxymoron
Rosenthaler Straße, 40/41
Mitte
☎ 28 39 18 85
Restaurant open every day from 11am.
In this former luxury hotel converted into a café, lounge, restaurant, bar and nightclub, young tenors in tails come every first Tuesday in the month to sing Italian arias to provide a musical accompaniment for your posta feasts. An unusual 'pasta opera' to go with a copious meal (DM50).

LIVELY ATMOSPHERE

Storch
Warburgerstraße, 54
☎ 784 20 59
Every day 6-11pm.
With its large wooden tables and enamel plates decorating the walls, this simple, convivial establishment is in reality one of the most renowned Alsatian restaurants in the city. Besides the delicious flambéed tarts, you'll be able to sample more elaborate dishes that'll make your mouth water just reading about the menu. A very good selection of wines.

Le Cochon Bourgeois
Fichtesstraße, 24
Kreuzberg
☎ 693 01 01
Mon.-Sat. 6-11.30pm.
In a relaxed setting, you'll find very convivial service and properly-prepared French dishes, all for a more than reasonable price (set meal DM60, drink included). Since the arrival of the new chef, the Cochon Bourgeois has quickly gained in popularity. It's a place to remember and one you can rely on.

Café Jolesh
Muskauer Straße, 1
Kreuzberg
☎ 612 35 81
Every day 10-1am.
Dark green walls, old red leather seats and large glass chandeliers define this Austrian restaurant frequented by the Kreuzberg art scene and local regulars. A very pleasant, spacious setting and much-prized inventive cuisine.

Pummarola
Grolmannstraße, 21
Charlottenburg
☎ 312 11 21
Every day noon-midnight,
Sun. 6pm.
Among the many restaurants in Grolmannsstrasse, this Italian establishment is perhaps one of the most convivial. Decorated in bright, colourful country fashion, it's a real little local restaurant where people come to eat traditional pasta or starters with a Southern Italian flavour.

Van Loo
Carl-Herz-Ufer, 5
☎ 692 62 93
Mon.-Sun. 10-1am.
This Dutch boat is the first to have opened as a restaurant on the delightful banks of the Landwehrkanal. The view from the boat is simply wonderful. If the restaurant seems a little cramped in summer, the terrace is an idyllic setting for a coffee or a tasty fish dish. The Josephine, which is moored alongside the Van Loo, offers buffet trips from April to October. Ask for more details.

RESTAURANTS

WHERE TO FIND GOOD CAKES

Café Lebensart
Unter den Linden, 69a
☎ 229 00 18
Every day 9am-midnight.
On the well-known avenue, Unter den Linden, between the Hotel Adlon and the Russian embassy, this is a good place to come for dessert. You'll find an amazing choice of fruit, cream and chocolate cakes and tarts. The ice creams are delicious, too.

Sowohl als auch
Kollwitzstraße, 88
☎ 442 93 11
🄵 448 13 82
Every day 9-2am.
A very trendy café in the Kiez district with an extremely friendly atmosphere and very pleasant decor. People come here to have coffee and above all to sample one of the delicious homemade cakes of the day. The cheesecakes (Käsekuchen) and poppyseed cakes (Mohnkuchen) are a real treat. Make sure you pay a visit if you're in the area.

Operncafé im Opernpalais
Unter den Linden, 5
☎ 20 26 83
Every day 9am-midnight.
Next to the Komprinzpalais, the Opernpalais – once known as the Prinzessinnenpalais (Princesses' Palace) – is a historic place where you can come for refreshments at the Königin Luise or Fridericus, for a beer or cocktail in the Opernschänke, or for delicious cakes in the Biedermeier setting of the Operncafé, where the cake counter is several metres long. In summer, the beer garden and terrace is a popular meeting-place.

Café Ephraim's
Spreeufer, 1
☎ 24 72 59 47
Every day 10am-midnight.
In the historic St Nicolas district, this tea room and restaurant will charm you with its unusual dining-room atmosphere. The house speciality, Ephraim's Haustorte is a tempting concoction of butter, cream and frangipani that's worth breaking your diet for. In summer, you can take advantage of the terrace on the banks of the Spree.

IMBISSE

Mäcky Messer
Mulackstraße, 29
Mitte
☎ 283 49 42
Tue.-Sat. 6pm-midnight.
In this charming little Imbiss in one of the most pleasant streets in Mitte, you can sample a whole range of sushi, as well as Japanese soups, salads and other fish dishes, all in a very relaxed drum'n'bass atmosphere.

Dada Falafel
Lienienstraße, 132
Mitte
☎ 282 83 17
Every day 11am-midnight.
An Imbiss with a pleasant decor where you can sustain yourself with tasty Lebanese doner kebabs or refresh yourself with freshly-squeezed fruit juice. The warm, friendly service is sure to make you want to come back.

Salomon Bagels
Joachimstaler Straße, 13
Charlottenburg
☎ 881 81 96
Mon.-Fri. 9am-8pm,
Sat. 10am-4pm.
A good place on the Ku'damm to sample these delicious traditional ring-shaped rolls. The bagels are very carefully prepared here, with a very varied choice of fillings, including cream cheese, avocado, tuna, tomato and mozzarella, to name but a few. A fresh, light snack that'll keep you going through the day.

Sachiko Sushi
Grolmannstraße, 47
Charlottenburg
☎ 313 22 82
Mon.-Sat. noon-midnight.
A little sushi bar with a very original concept and design. Small baguettes filled with sushi float on a boat-shaped counter and it's up to you to fish out whatever you want. A plate of sushi costs DM18 and you can have as much tea as you like.

IMBISSE

BEER GARDENS AND CAFÉS

Prater Biergarten
Kastanienallee, 7-9
Prenzlauer Berg
☎ 448 56 88
Mon.-Fri. 6pm-1am.
The beer garden and café of Prenzlauer Berg is an institution. As long ago as 1852, there were open-air performances of songs and operettas here. Later, it was the place where August Bebel and Rosa Luxemburg made their declarations. Today, after restoration, the Prater has retained its legendary concert hall and its beer garden remains a popular and convivial meeting-place.

Pfefferber Biergarten
Schönhauser Allee, 176
Prenzlauer Berg
☎ 449 65 34
Beer garden open
May-Sep., every day
from 10am.
The Pfefferberg is a former brewery that was converted some time ago into a cultural centre and renowned concert hall. On the first floor, there's a pleasantly shady summer garden where you can have breakfast, drink beer or sample grills at the end of the day. It's an important meeting-place of the Prenzlauer Berg alternative scene.

Kleine Orangerie
Spandauer Damm, 20
Charlottenburg
☎ 322 20 21
In winter, every day.
10am-8pm,
in summer, every day.
10am-10pm.
This is the ideal place to come to relax after visiting Charlottenburg Palace. As you rest in the winter garden or in the shade of the trees, you can enjoy a slice of cake or, if you're very hungry, something more substantial.

Café Adler
Friedrichstraße, 206
Mitte/Kreuzberg
☎ 251 89 65
Every day from 9am-midnight.
This legendary café near the East-West crossing point, Checkpoint Charlie, was where travellers came to exchange impressions after visiting East Berlin. It's a historic place on several levels since this former chemist's is considered to be the oldest house in Kreuzberg. Aside from its past, the café is nowadays the nicest place to meet and relax in the district.

Kafka
Oranienstraße, 204
Kreuzberg
☎ 612 24 29
Every day 8.30am-11.30pm.
A recently-renovated Kreuzberg Kneipe and, since its reopening, a place much appreciated for its relaxed atmosphere, good, cheap cuisine and shady garden. Especially recommended for its varied and abundant buffet breakfast (DM15.50 per person).

Weyers
Pariser Straße, 16
☎ 881 93 78
Every day 8-1am.
A simple local café-restaurant with a fine setting on the charming Ludwigkirchplatz and a very pleasant terrace in summer. You can also enjoy well-prepared and reasonably-priced dishes here.

BARS AND CLUBS

Harry's New York Bar
Lützowufer, 15 (in the Esplanade hotel)
Tiergarten
☎ 254 78 21
Every day from noon.
In the setting of the luxury Esplanade hotel, Harry's was long considered one of the finest bars in Berlin. While the location and its decor now seem dated, the bar is still a great classic.

Paris 15 Cocktails
Pariser Straße, 15
Wilmersdorf
☎ 881 87 51
Every day from 10pm.
Not far from Lurwigkircheplatz, a cocktail bar with a very classy decor that has recently become extremely fashionable. The bar owes its success to its cocktails, which may be rather pricey (DM20), but which taste fantastic. Try the Himbeer-Daiquiri (raspberry) and the Coconut Kiss – they're quite delicious.

Newton Bar
Charlottenstraße, 57
Mitte
☎ 20 61 29 99
🖷 20 29 54 25
Every day 6pm-late.
With its magnificent bar jutting out into the street, this brand-new Gendarmenmarkt bar is probably going to become one of the smartest places in Berlin. People come here before or after a show to have a glass of champagne or smoke a cigar in the cigar lounge on the first floor. Hiring your own cigar locker is obviously a must (DM400 a year). On the walls hang the colossal pictures of nudes by the German photographer Helmut Newton.

Mitte Bar
Oranienburgerstraße, 46
Mitte
☎ 283 38 37
Every day from 10am.
A pleasant, rather smart bar in the liveliest in-street in Mitte. The clientele is fairly trendy and cosmopolitan, with DJs at the weekend.

Jubinal
Angle Augustraße/
Tucholskystraße
Mitte
☎ 28 38 73 77
Every day from 7pm.
This Mitte bar with a 1970s atmosphere is a very pleasant place little frequented by tourists. People come here for a beer, a cocktail or a glass of excellent wine and to spend a quiet evening relaxing and listening to the sound of jazz (regular concerts).

Zoulu Bar
Haupstraße, 3
Schöneberg
☎ 784 17 17
Every day from 8pm.
With its red leather seats, office lamps and many photos hanging on the wall, the Zoulu is one of the most frequented bars in Schöneberg. A student clientele gathers here at the weekend to

drink the delicious Zoulu cocktails (try the rasta killer or the zombie) and, later, to dance to the soul, acid jazz, funk or hip hop mixes of the D.Js.

Diener
Grolmanstraße, 47
Charlottenburg
☎ 881 53 29
Every day from 6pm
This bar-restaurant, which bears the name of a great boxer of the 1920s, is an institution. For years, it has attracted theatre actors, who come here to be seen or have supper after the performance. It's probably because of its old-fashioned charm and patina that the Diener continues to be one of the favourite places of theatre people.

Bierhimmel
Oranienstraße, 181
Kreuzberg
☎ 615 31 22
Every day 2pm-3am, bar Wed.-Sat. from 9pm.
A typical Kneipe which is much frequented by the Kreuzberg 'scene', with yellow walls, old glass chandeliers and mirrors. From Wednesday onwards, the opening of the bar, with its equally original decor, livens up the atmosphere.

Roses
Oranienstraße, 187
Kreuzberg
☎ 615 65 70
Every day from 10pm.
One of the bars with a wild, kitsch decor that Berlin does so well. Frequented by a gay and lesbian clientele, Roses is a place you should visit to round off the evening.

Schlot
Kastanienallee, 29
☎ 448 21 60
Every day from 8pm.
In the heart of the alternative scene of Prenzlauer Berg, in a second rear courtyard, a room with a fireplace and a small stage hosts original jazz and cabaret shows.

Oxymoron
Rosenthaler Straße, 40/41
Mitte
☎ 283 91 886
From 11pm.
In the first inner courtyard of the Hackeschen Höfe, a former luxury hotel has been converted into a lounge and restaurant in the daytime and a rather smart nightclub after dark. Cosy and retro, it makes an original setting for dancing to House, hip hop, disco, soul and funk.

Kurvenstar
Angle Große/kleine Präsidentenstraße
Mitte
☎ 285 99 71-0
Every day from 9pm.
A recent newcomer to this chic, trendy corner of Mitte, the Kurvenstar is a bar, exotic restaurant and club rolled into one. Despite a mix of hip hop and soul music and an original 1970s decor, the atmosphere is often fairly subdued. Worth watching.

SO 36
Oranienstraße, 190
Kreuzberg
☎ 614 01 306
Mon.-Sat. from 10pm,
Sun. from 5pm.
A major meeting-place of the punk, alternative and gay scene in the eighties, now reserved for a gay and lesbian clientele on Wednesdays, with very varied evenings that are open to all, as well as regular concerts.

Sage Club
Brückenstraße, 1, in the Heinrich-Heine Straße U-Bahn station
Mitte
Thu.-Sun. from 11pm.
This club, formerly the Boogaloo Groove Station, was once the mecca of Berlin hip hop. Recently refurbished, it's now known as the Sage Club. The decor may be interesting but the atmosphere is overrated and the music anything but original. It doesn't matter, though, because, after a certain time of day, the Sage becomes the in-place to end the night.

A WALK AMONG THE GALLERIES

Shortly after the fall of the Wall, a whole new generation of galleries opened in the old East Berlin district of Mitte. In a few short years, their young, ambitious owners have breathed new life into the Berlin art scene. Compared with the galleries in the east of the city, those in the west seem staid and traditional. The east is where you'll find the rising young stars of contemporary art, while the west is home to the great names of the 20th century.

Galerie Brusberg
Kurfürstendamm, 213
Charlottenburg
☎ 882 76 82
Tue.-Fri. 10am-6.30pm,
Sat. 10am-2pm.
After forty years in the business, Dieter Brusberg is considered the number one art dealer in Berlin. His favourite area is Surrealism and Dadaism. Apart from these movements, he's also known for having encouraged and promoted artists from the former GDR.

Galerie Volker Diehl
Niebuhrstraße 2
Charlottenburg
☎ 881 82 80
Tue.-Fri. 2-6.30pm,
Sat. 11am-2pm.
Volker Diehl is one of the organisers and directors of Berlin's celebrated contemporary art fair. In his gallery, you'll find works by Andy Warhol, Donald Judd, Markus Lüpertz and Georg Baselitz. Besides the great names, Volker Diehl also shows young international artists.

Galerie Pels-Leusden
Fasanenstraße, 25
Charlottenburg
☎ 885 91 50
Mon.-Fri. 11am-6.30pm,
Sat. 11am-2pm.
A gallery which has presented the great classic trends of modern art for over 50 years – Impressionists, Expressionists and artists of the new objectivity.

Galerie Franck + Schulte
Mommenstraße, 56
Charlottenburg
☎ 324 00 44
Mon.-Fri. 11am-6pm,
Sat. 11am-4pm.
A gallery specialising in conceptual and minimalist art housing regular one-man shows by the great names of the German contemporary art scene, such as R. Horn and K. Sieverding.

Galerie Michael Schultz
Mommsenstraße, 34
Charlottenburg
☎ 324 15 91
Tue.-Fri. 2-7pm,
Sat. 10am-2pm.
Since the late 1970s, Michael Schultz has been a major player on the Berlin art scene. In his gallery, there are works by the artists who were dubbed neo-Expressionists in the 1980s (A.R. Penk, Fetting, Baselitz, etc.) and unknown young artists.

Arndt & Partner
Augustraße 35
Mitte
☎ 280 81 23
Tue.-Sat. noon-6pm.
This was one of the first galleries to risk coming to the eastern district of Mitte in 1994. The gallery's ambitious young manager, Matthias Arndt, has chosen well-known international artists, such as Sophie Calle and Thomas Hirschhorn, as well as the rising young stars of the art world. Besides exhibitions, there are regular readings in the Labor (basement).

Galerie Eigen + Art.
Auguststraße, 26
Mitte
☎ 28880 66 05
Tue.-Fri. 2-7pm,
Sat. 11am-5pm.
In Leipzig, Harry Lybke was one of the few private gallery owners in the GDR. When he arrived in Berlin in 1992, he was already something of a legend. His strong point was young German

and international artists, most of whom were living and working in Berlin.

S.S.K.
Lienienstraße, 158
☎ 28 38 64 64
Wed.-Sat. 2-8pm.
'Collect art!', is this young gallery's motto. S.S.K. sells humorous and occasionally irreverent works, mostly by Berlin artists, at very affordable prices (DM1-1,000).

Galerie Klosterfelde
Lienienstraße 160
Mitte
☎ 283 53 05
Tue.-Sat. 11am-6pm.
Although one of the youngest in Mitte, the owner of the gallery is already a professional who has studied in New York. High-quality works by internationally-renowned artists (Dan Peterman, John Bock and Steven Pipin)

Galerie Wohnmaschine
Tucholsky Straße, 36
Mitte
☎ 30 87 20. 15
Tue.-Fri. 2-7pm,
Sat. noon-5pm.
Friedrich Loock is a pioneer among East Berliners since he turned his Mitte flat into a gallery as long ago as 1988. Since then, he has specialised in the discovery of talented young Berliners (York de Knöfel, Florian Merkel and Anton Henning), with Japanese artists (Niwa Yanagi and Yoshiro Suda) and photography also on the menu.

Galerie Neugerriemschneider
Lienienstraße, 155
Mitte
☎ 30 87 28 10
Tue.-Sat. 11am-6pm.
A young pair hailing from Cologne, a fine exhibition space and the latest artists (Wolfgang Tillmans, Rikrit Tiravanija and Elizabeth Peyton).

A WALK IN POTSDAM

To get to Potsdam, take the S-Bahn at Zoologischer Garten, in the direction of Potsdam and get off at Potsdam Stadt station. Once the residence town of the Prussian kings, Potsdam is the Berliners' favourite excursion destination. Besides its famous palace and park, people come here to see the Dutch quarter of the old town, the Russian colony and the famous DEFA studios in Neubabelsberg. Among the many possible walks, the one through Sanssouci Palace is definitely the nicest. To get to Park Sanssouci, the quickest and most pleasant way to go is through the town. On leaving the S-Bahn, make your way down Friedrich-Ebert-strasse. When you come to the corner of the pedestrian street, Brandenburgerstraße, take the left fork in the direction of the Brandenburg Gate. Go north up Schopenhauer Straße, which will take you to the main entrance, the Obelisk Portal. You'll find yourself in the Hauptallee, the majestic central walk leading to the New Palace. On your left, you'll catch sight of the Friedens-kirche, the funerary church that Friedrich Wilhelm IV had built for himself on the Italian model of a paleo-Christian basilica. As you make your way up the walk, the Sanssouci Palace will appear before you. The plans of this modestly-sized but sumptuous residence were drawn up by Friedrich the Great himself. Designed as a place of pleasure and amusement, this Rococo retreat was used to entertain many of the diplomats, writers (such as Voltaire), philosophers and artists with whom the king love to surround himself. The famous library, the music room and the marble hall are worth visiting in themselves (guided tours leave every 20 minutes and last about an hour). From the terrace, you'll have a fine view of the magnificent park laid out in the 19th century by Peter Joseph Lenné. On your left, you'll see the Bildergalerie, which was the first gallery in Europe built exclusively to **house a collection of paintings.** Recently renovated, it contains works by Italian and Flemish painters (Van Dyck, Rubens and Tintoretto). The long building on your right was originally the Orangery. It was later turned into guest houses and renamed Neue Kammern (new rooms). If you go round the palace to the back, you'll discover an elegant semicircular colonnade and, in the distance on a hill, the Ruinenberg (Ruin Mountain), with its mock-ruined amphitheatre and ancient temple. These were designed to hide the water reserves that once fed the fountains, a complex system that never actually worked. You'll then arrive at the remains of an old windmill (Historische Mühle), that has a famous story attached to it. Annoyed by the noise of the sails, Friedrich II tried to evict the owner. When the matter was taken to court and the miller won, the king was forced to respect the judgement in order to uphold the law. A few metres/yards away stands the New Orangery. One of the rooms houses copies of works by Raphael. If you feel like a rest, make for the Café im Drachenhaus, a small pagoda that has been turned into a tea room. If you aren't tired, you can head back to the central walk and on to the New Palace, a gigantic late Rococo building you'll either love or hate. Among the ostentatiously-decorated rooms, the palace possesses a grotto encrusted with coral and shells (guided tours only). If you want to continue your walk, carry on south and you'll come across two masterpieces by Schinkel. These little gems forming a picturesque mixed group were built according to sketches by Friedrich Wilhelm IV and display the king's passionate love of Italy. Both Charlottenhof Palace, a residence with complex , elegant neo-Classical architecture, and the Roman baths (Römische Bäder) were designed to harmonise with the English park laid out by Peter Joseph Lenné. When you reach this point, you've almost come to the end of your walk. All that remains is for you to make your way to the Chinese Tea House, an 18th-century folly, before heading for Marly Garden and the Friedenskirche. You then simply take the exit to get back to the Brandenburg Gate.

HACHETTE TRAVEL GUIDES

Titles available in this series:

A GREAT WEEKEND IN AMSTERDAM (ISBN: 1 84202 002 1)
A GREAT WEEKEND IN BARCELONA (ISBN: 1 84202 005 6)
A GREAT WEEKEND IN FLORENCE (ISBN: 1 84202 010 2)
A GREAT WEEKEND IN LONDON (ISBN: 1 84202 013 7)
A GREAT WEEKEND IN NAPLES (ISBN: 1 84202 016 1)
A GREAT WEEKEND IN NEW YORK (ISBN: 1 84202 004 8)
A GREAT WEEKEND IN PARIS (ISBN: 1 84202 001 3)
A GREAT WEEKEND IN PRAGUE (ISBN: 1 84202 000 5)
A GREAT WEEKEND IN ROME (ISBN: 1 84202 003 X)
A GREAT WEEKEND IN BERLIN (ISBN: 1 84202 061 7)
A GREAT WEEKEND IN BRUSSELS (ISBN: 1 84202 017 X)
A GREAT WEEKEND IN VIENNA (ISBN: 1 84202 026 9)

Publication Autumn 2000
A GREAT WEEKEND IN VENICE (ISBN: 1 84202 018 8)

HACHETTE VACANCES
Who better to write about France than the French?
A series of colourful, information-packed, leisure and activity guides fo
family holidays by French authors. Literally hundreds of suggestions fo
things to do and sights to see per title.

BRITTANY (ISBN: 1 84202 007 2)
LANGUEDOC-ROUSSILLON (ISBN: 1 84202 008 0)
POITOU-CHARENTES (ISBN: 1 84202 009 9)
PROVENCE & THE COTE D'AZUR (ISBN: 1 84202 006 4)
PYRENEES & GASCONY (ISBN: 1 84202 015 3)
SOUTH-WEST FRANCE (ISBN: 1 84202 014 5)

ROUTARD
Comprehensive and reliable guides offering insider advice for the
independent traveller, starting Autumn 2000.

ANDALUCIA (ISBN: 1 84202 028 5)
BELGIUM (ISBN: 1 84202 022 6)
BRITTANY (ISBN: 1 84202 020 X)
CALIFORNIA, NEVADA & ARIZONA (ISBN: 1 84202 025 0)
CUBA (ISBN: 1 84202 062 5)
GREEK ISLANDS & ATHENS (ISBN: 1 84202 023 4)
IRELAND (ISBN: 1 84202 024 2)
PARIS (ISBN: 1 84202 027 7)
PROVENCE & THE COTE D'AZUR (ISBN: 1 84202 019 6)
SOUTHERN ITALY, ROME & SICILY (ISBN: 1 84202 021 8)
THAILAND (ISBN: 1 84202 029 3)
WEST CANADA & ONTARIO (ISBN: 1 84202 031 5)